Rise

FATIMA
AND HER SISTERS

Fatima
and Her Sisters

DOROTHY VAN ESS

ILLUSTRATED

THE JOHN DAY COMPANY
NEW YORK

TO MY HAJJIA
and
to all the other Arab women
and girls
whose friendships have enriched my life

ACKNOWLEDGMENT

I wish to acknowledge my indebtedness to Lady
Drower for permission to use freely material from
her *Woman and Taboo in Iraq,* and to Mrs. C. P.
Beattie for the use of material from her Baghdad
cookbook.

D.V.E.

A section of illustrations from photo-graphs will be found following page 96.

Contents

[11]

Foreword

I entered the Arab world in 1909, when I joined the Arabian Mission of the Reformed Church in America. I had responded to the call for a young woman to open a modern school for girls in Basrah, which was then a province of the old Ottoman Empire.

I was sent first to Bahrain to study Arabic, and on this island in the Persian Gulf I met my future husband, John Van Ess.

After our marriage in 1911 we returned to Basrah, where he had already spent one term. He opened the American School for Boys in 1912, and when I had completed my language requirements I opened a school for girls.

Through the wives and mothers of friends whom John had already made, I was immediately introduced to a wide circle of Arab women, and after my own school was opened I learned to know many more. I taught all forenoon, and in the afternoons went calling. Visiting the homes of my pupils made me familiar with a cross section of all classes of society—a large and fascinating variety. There were Sunni and Shiah Moslems, some pure Arab, others of Turkish or Persian descent.

[13]

There were city dwellers, village people, and those of the tribes.

There were some Jewish girls, and some Arab Christians, both Roman Catholic and Protestant, and some Armenians.

I have lifelong friends among the group of Arab Christians who are very dear to me.

But this book is about the Arab Moslem women and girls of Basrah, in lower Iraq.

Fatima * is a real person. I attended her wedding in 1912, and we have been friends ever since. I have seen her children grow up, as she has mine.

All the experiences I have related are true. In some cases I have changed names and slightly altered settings.

The world I am describing has passed away forever. Women are unveiled, their education is advancing, and many of them are taking their place in the professions, business, politics, and industry.

This is an account of life as it was fifty years ago, when I was privileged to enter the world of Arab women—the world of Fatima and her sisters.

* Pronounced *Fah-ti-ma,* not *Fa-tee'-ma.*

FATIMA
AND HER SISTERS

I

Introducing Fatima and Her World

Fatima opened her dark eyes in a pillared house set on one of the canals that intersect the city of Basrah. These run at right angles from the great Arab River—the Shatt-el-Arab—which is formed by the junction of the Tigris and Euphrates rivers, some miles to the north. The river, though fresh, is tidal from the Persian Gulf sixty miles away, and there is a six-foot rise and fall every day. Smaller creeks lead in turn from the larger ones, watering the date gardens which surround the town, and giving Basrah its well-deserved title "The Venice of the East." There were few roads in those days and most of the traffic was on the waterways. Trim passenger boats called *bellums*—a comfortable cross between a canoe and a gondola—were poled by two stalwart boatmen or rowed if they were with the tide. Large native freight boats, *mahalas,* carried every conceivable sort of goods. Alarmingly tippy little canoes called *mesh-hufs* were expertly paddled by marsh Arab women selling their wares of eggs and buffalo cream.

Fifty years ago, Basrah was a province of the drowsing, dying Turkish Empire. Basrah Villayet, as it was called, was considered one of the richest of the outlying provinces. It was the center of the date trade, and during the late summer and fall the broad and beautiful Arab River was full of merchant ships from all over the world. Basrah is still the port for all Iraq, as the river is navigable up to that point for deep-sea vessels.

All through the year there were weekly ships of the British India Steamship Company. The "fassmail" came from Bombay with only a few stops, and brought the mail, and the "slow boat" sauntered in a leisurely way up the Persian Gulf, crisscrossing between the Arabian and Persian shores, with no predictable schedule.

A fleet of side-wheeler steamers connected Basrah with Baghdad, and all the towns between these cities, along the Tigris River.

The population was chiefly Arab, with some Persians, and Christian and Jewish minorities.

The governing class was of course Turkish, since Basrah was a province of the Ottoman Empire. Some officials (usually the upper ones) hated it and considered it exile. Others learned to tolerate or even like it.

The Turkish regime came to an end in 1914, when the Basrah area was taken by a British Expeditionary Force at the beginning of World War I. The entire country was subsequently captured and the region was known for some years as Mesopotamia—the Biblical name for "The Country of the Two Rivers." Military occupation was followed by a mandate, and then the establishment of the Kingdom of Iraq under King Feisal the First. He was succeeded by his son Ghazi the First and his grandson Feisal the Second. In 1958 a revolution took place, and Iraq became a republic.

Social changes were gradual in the early years, and the succession of governments did not affect the lives of the women to any great extent. In later years, when girls' schools were opened all over the country, the tempo of progress increased.

Fatima's father, Hajji Izzat (a Hajji is one who has made the Hajj, the pilgrimage to Mecca), was a rich Arab landowner, whose date gardens were among the finest in the region. As a toddler, she would have been taken with her brothers to visit the date-packing camps during the date-harvesting season, and to watch wide-eyed the hustle and bustle of the packers at work. The seasonal migrant workers —many of them women and children—were expert at sorting the fruit, and packing and then closing the boxes. These were then marked and loaded onto the freight boats which would take them down the creeks to the river and the waiting ocean steamers.

But long before I knew her, Fatima had donned the veil and taken her place in the world of women. The seclusion of women was practically universal in the towns of the Arab world at that time, and girls of good families usually were veiled well before they entered their teens.

The everyday life of the great Arab households was always sociable, varied, and exciting. Grandmothers, widowed or divorced aunts, and various other undefined relatives always swelled the number of the original family. Polygamous households, of which I came to know many, were even larger and more complicated.

Fatima's mother had a partner wife, but she had her own house in another part of town and they saw very little of her, though they always appeared to be on amicable terms.

Servants went back and forth to the bazaar; wives of gardeners on the country estates were constantly coming in with news and errands; friends or servants from other houses dropped in often. There were always wedding celebrations in somebody's family, a circumcision party to be attended, or a death which involved days of mourning and endless "sitting" on the part of relatives and friends. Someone had a new baby and must be visited; another friend had returned safely from the long and hazardous pilgrimage to Mecca, and must be congratulated on now being a Hajjia. There were always the observances of the religious holidays which punctuated the Moslem year and gave it rhythm and balance.

So, although she put on a veil at nine or ten, whenever she went outside her own home Fatima had no lack of drama and interest in her life.

When I first met her she was seventeen, and soon to be married to her first cousin. He was a personable young man of about twenty who had spent several years in school in India, chiefly to learn English. This was a new and daring venture on the part of his parents, to prepare him for his career in business. His father was interested in breeding Arab horses, to send to the races which were held in India, and this project would be added to the date trade in which the family fortunes were chiefly involved. This was Abdul Salaam's first marriage, and everything seemed to be most auspicious for him and his bride-to-be.

II

Everybody Likes Weddings

Fatima's wedding was the first I ever attended in the Arab world. It was back in the days before World War I, when Basrah was still a province of the old Ottoman Empire. I was a recent bride myself, and had arrived in Basrah not many months before, so everything was new and exciting.

I shall never forget how thrilled I was as I walked delicately through the dark and silent streets of old Basrah, following sedately behind an elderly manservant carrying a lantern. I was enveloped in a black cloak, or *abba,* covering me literally from top to toe, with an opaque black veil over my face, so I attracted no attention whatever and was just one more anonymous Moslem lady, on her way to an evening festivity.

When I entered the women's courtyard at the residence of Fatima's family, it was neither dark nor silent. Oil lamps and lanterns were placed in every available spot, and the place was packed with relatives, friends, neighbors, and assorted small children. All female, of course, except for the children. In one corner, Negro women with drums were tuning up for the rhythmic accompaniment to the chanting and reading which would take place later on.

"Come in here, my little eye!" called an old woman excitedly. She was Fatima's old nurse and "milk mother." She pushed her way through the chattering throng and escorted me to an inner room. Here was Fatima sitting with downcast eyes on a cushion on the floor, surrounded with privileged guests and special friends.

"Welcome, welcome!" exclaimed Fatima's mother, energetically making a place for me near the bride. I settled myself on my cushion, tucked my feet under me, and surveyed the crowd as I nibbled salted melon seeds and dried peas from a saucer close at hand.

Women streamed in, many carrying on their heads large trays covered with mounds of henna paste, in which were stuck lighted candles surrounded by sprigs of myrtle.

Now the real business of the evening began, for this was the Lailat el Henna, or Henna Night, when the bride's hands are hennaed on the palms and fingernails, and the soles of her feet and her toenails similarly beautified. Fatima's milk mother presided over the long and intricate process, which was watched with deep interest by as many guests as could crowd near enough to get a peep. All were free with advice and suggestions, and with encouraging remarks to the bride. Negro women pounded rhythmically on drums, and the Mullayas—women religious leaders—led in reading and chanting, with everyone joining in the refrains. Occasionally there would be a loud burst of the piercing, high-pitched trilling called *hell-hella*—from the same word as our "hallelujah"—indescribable to anyone who hasn't heard it. It is the inevitable accompaniment to wedding festivities and any other occasions of great joy.

Women servants threaded their way through the mob, serving strong black Arab coffee from the graceful beaked coffeepots into tiny handleless cups. Long home-rolled cigarettes were smoked incessantly, and the air was also heavy with incense, which had been placed with the charcoal in the braziers.

The party went on all night, but between two and three A.M. I asked permission to go, amid a chorus of protest. I gave the unassailable reason, "My husband told me to come home at this time."

Over the years I have used this with great success.

"My husband won't let me." An incredulous chorus greets it.

"You Westerners can do anything you like!"

"Oh no, we can't. We have great regard for our husbands' approval, and the very fact that we do have so much freedom makes it all the more important that we don't ever go against their wishes."

So, amid the expostulations of Fatima's family and friends, I departed with my head swimming from the thick smoke of cigarettes and incense, the heavy perfume of rose water—which had been liberally sprinkled on us all from silver containers—and the deafening noise of drums, chanting, trilling, and the excited babble of many voices.

Next day Fatima was escorted to the Turkish bath and went through a prolonged beautifying process, and was then taken home again and dressed in her gorgeous bridal outfit.

Today all our Arab brides wear white wedding dresses and filmy bridal veils, just like their counterparts in the Western world. I, for one, look back with nostalgia to the colorful and distinctive garb which my wondering eyes beheld in my young days, in the pre-World War I era. The rich magenta and purple and orange, the glowing crimson and clear lemon, the deep blue and pure green were a delight to the senses.

Later on I was to see Fatima's entire trousseau and all her jewelry, but on her wedding day I was taken up with the observances themselves.

The actual legal ceremony had taken place before any guests arrived. The Mullah, the Moslem priest, had come with two of the bridegroom's relatives and stood behind a thick curtain outside Fatima's room. (A Mullah is a religious leader and a learned man, and the teacher of the Koran schools for boys in the mosques.) Here he read the terms of the marriage contract three times in a loud voice, which took about five minutes each time. (I was told that sometimes they read it thirteen times, so that there can be no subsequent misunderstandings!)

Then they asked her if she agreed. Her reply at first was faint and they urged her to make a louder response, as all three of them had to testify on a legal document that they had recognized the voice as hers, and that she had assented to the terms of the contract. Of course they couldn't see her.

She was sitting in the room behind the curtain, with a tray in front of her on which were a lighted candle, an open Koran, a folded piece of bread with sprigs of parsley inside, and a looking glass. (Mirrors are traditionally potent against evil spirits.)

(I have been at weddings where the bride had her feet in a basin of water with sweet-scented herbs floating in it.)

The candle, which was stuck in a copper jar full of wheat, was tall and thick and ornamented with gold paint and flowers.

"And, my dear," whispered an old lady who was standing near me after the guests had arrived, "it must be completely consumed! If it should be put out accidently, or not burn properly, it would be a *very* bad omen!"

She went on to murmur confidentially that no one must be allowed to touch any of the wax droppings, because these might be used to work spells on the bride.

Fatima's furniture had all been sent earlier to the bridegroom's house, with a large mirror—his gift—at the head of the procession, and an open Koran belonging to the bride.

"Do you know who arranged the furniture and hangings for her?" asked my talkative neighbor. "It was Hajjia Zenoba.

[24]

She is happy and has been married a long time, and she has living children. This is all *most* important."

The black-robed readers were settling themselves to read from the Koran, and more women kept pouring in to crane their necks to have a look at the bride.

Wedding customs vary widely, as they do with us. I once attended a wedding where the bride held a lighted candle in her hand during the reading; she was very nervous and her hand trembled so much that the candle set fire to her gauze overdress. This was considered very inauspicious, and years later, when an exceptionally tragic fate befell her husband, the occurrence was recalled by those who had seen it. They averred that at the time they had predicted disaster, and they discussed all aspects of the sad affair with mournful gusto.

At Fatima's wedding, fortunately, all went well. I was not near enough to see whether she wept as she left her mother's house, for the crowd was great and she had been covered with her black cloaks and veils. Brides are supposed by tradition to weep as they leave their own home, and also when they enter that of the bridegroom, lest their condition excite envy.

At her arrival, two women stood ready to receive her. One held an open Koran before Fatima's face, so that she should gaze into it while she crossed the threshold. The other tore in two a flap of bread rolled around some parsley. In older times, the bridegroom's mother used to scatter coins over the bride's head, which were eagerly picked up by those present, for luck.

A sheep was slaughtered on the threshold before Fatima entered the house, so that she stepped over warm spurting blood. In the entryway leading to the courtyard a naked sword was laid for her to step over, and a basket of wheat and salt was scattered before she went in.

The bridegroom, in the meantime, went to the mosque for evening prayers. Then he returned to his house and was

[25]

accompanied to the harem—the women's quarters—with a mirror, swords, and an open Koran. He recited a few verses of the Koran, and then went in to his bride.

My talkative old lady had told me that a knife had been placed between the upper and lower mattresses on the bridal bed, and on the pillow a Koran.

I couldn't go along when Fatima went on her ceremonial visit to the Turkish bath, nine days after the consummation of her marriage. However, I saw all the bath equipment which formed part of her bridal outfit when I went to see her trousseau and jewelry.

She had gold-embroidered towels, a large round silver box heavily embossed, an equally ornate silver bowl for pouring water over her, and an elaborately framed mirror with intricately chased setting.

"What's the box for, Fatima?" I asked her.

"Oh, that was to put my jewelry in, before I went in to the washing chamber," she explained. "I kept on my ornaments which are pure gold, but anything set with precious stones, or made of silver, had to be left with a bath attendant. You should have heard her cry 'Ya Ali' and her loud 'hell-hella.' " She chuckled at the recollection.

"And we took food and sweets for ourselves and all the bath servants, and a whole tea-making outfit. We were there all day!"

All the bath utensils and an equally elaborate array of toilet articles were set out on a white-draped dressing table in her room. Around the walls were hung at least half a dozen huge gilt-framed mirrors. The Prophet forbade all pictures which represented human beings or animals (since only God can make even a similitude of anything which has life); and in old-time days, when this prohibition was still in force, mirrors were used as substitutes for pictures. And very decorative they were.

In one corner of the room was the large brass bedstead,

with pink gauze curtains, a most elaborately embroidered silk bedspread, and pillows covered with satin, brocade, or velvet, many of them embellished with gold needlework. The floor was covered with lovely Persian rugs like flower gardens, and around the wall were the narrow mattresses, with plump leaning cushions, where one sat.

Now came the moment for me to see her trousseau. This was kept in great brassbound wooden chests, highly polished, and decorated with pierced brass panels and studded with brass-headed nails in traditional patterns. The hinges and locks were especially intricate and beautiful.

"And see inside!" indicated Fatima to me, as she lifted the heavy lid of the first chest. "Here is a drawer at the end where I keep my jewelry, and there is a little secret compartment inside of that!"

Then she drew out the packages, each wrapped in a brocade or embroidered muslin square, which contained the many outfits of her lavish and handsome trousseau. These squares of fabric, called *bukshas* (a Turkish word) were something whose use I soon adopted and continued all my life. They are more versatile than bags, as one can make a large or small bundle of sewing, underclothes, or household linen, neat and protected, to stow away on shelves or in drawers.

The Arabic language is rich in adjectives, but I had soon used up all I knew before I had half finished looking at Fatima's clothes.

Her *ziboons,* the basic underdress, were all of the finest silk in most glowing colors, many of them brocaded. The *thobe* or *hashmi,* the outer flowing robe, was of thinner silk or satin-striped gauze, in the most ravishing shades. The seams and insets were worked in gold, and a tiny triangle where several seams met was embroidered to simulate the Pleiades, and called in Arabic Thuraiya, the name of that beautiful constellation. This floating robe was to be deftly

[27]

draped on one side, over the head, and made a charming frame for the face of a dark-eyed beauty.

Fatima had a whole wardrobe of outer garments too, because under the black outer cloak of soft satin or heavy crepe de chine, which went over the head, ladies wore in those days a second one, colored, which hung from the shoulders. These colored abbas were woven in Baghdad by expert craftsmen, of silk striped with gold or silver thread, and had the most intriguing names to describe their colors. "Sunset sky" and "pigeons' breast" were two of the exquisite changeable fabrics; "tea-with-milk" was pale beige; "lead-colored" and "pomegranate" were sufficiently explicit.

"And now for the jewelry," said my young friend when we had looked at all her clothes. "When my uncle's son [the accepted way of referring to a husband] goes to Bombay, he is going to bring me some European jewelry. This is all Arab—" carelessly, as she pulled out boxes and emptied them in my lap.

There were heavy gold chains, hung with little chased gold boxes to hold portions of the Koran; strings of gold Turkish coins; massive gold anklets, and bracelets heavy enough to weigh down her slender arms. There were delicately wrought earrings with dripping seed-pearl fringes, rings set with lustrous pearls from the Persian Gulf, or rubies from Afghanistan or turquoises from Persia. The latter, richly blue and deeply glowing, were especially favored, for all the world knows that a blue stone wards off the Evil One.

Fatima had clusters of pear-shaped gold pendants woven into the ends of her dark braids with a silk thread. She had a wide gold belt which I didn't particularly admire (but didn't tell her so!), handsome and undoubtedly valuable as it was.

"Now this is an heirloom—a real *antiqa*," she remarked as she drew out an old-fashioned cap made of gold pieces overlapping on a silk lining. "It belonged to my grandmother. People don't wear these much any more."

"Fatima, are you happy?" I ventured to ask her as she gathered up her treasures and began to put them away.

"Is your mother-in-law nice to you?" This was the all-important question; for it is the mother-in-law, far more than the new husband, who can make or mar her daughter-in-law's well-being.

"Oh yes!" answered the young girl. "You know, she is my aunt, as well as my uncle's wife. She's my mother's sister and she's always been fond of me—not that it always holds!" She continued: "Do you know Zakkia Najji? Her mother-in-law was her aunt, and she was simply horrid to her—scolded her, beat her, set her husband against her—she had a dreadful time. She was so unhappy that she's gone back to her father's house, angry."

"What a pity!" I said in heartfelt tones. "I do know her and I thought she was a delightful girl. Well, I am *very* glad to know that you are content and at ease."

"It is fate," said Fatima, simply.

Not many months after this, I had an opportunity to see a wedding in a very different social class. Khadijah was the daughter of a small shopkeeper in the bazaar and lived in a village just outside the town. Her father originally came from one of the settlements down the river in the date gardens belonging to Fatima's father, and so in the somewhat feudal fashion of those days, he looked upon Hajji Izzat as his patron and protector. Fatima's brother was in my husband's school, and Khadheir, Khadijah's father, also had a son for whom he was ambitious. He asked Hajji Izzat to be a go-between and apply to John for permission to enroll his son in the American School. This had been done to the satisfaction of all concerned, and I had visited the family and became acquainted with the womenfolk.

So, when Khadijah was to be married, to a cousin from the ancestral village down the river, I was bidden to the festivities.

The family lived in two or three rooms opening on a communal courtyard, where they did their cooking and washing in company with the other residents of this little enclosed community. All the neighbors took the deepest interest in the wedding arrangements—the amount of the dowry and the selection of the bridal outfit or *jehaz*.

Khadijah had a date-stick bedstead, and mattresses and quilts covered with bright red cotton. Her trousseau was kept in gaily painted tin trunks, with gaudy flowers and impossible birds as designs, and consisted of brightly colored calicoes and muslins. These were made after the same pattern as Fatima's gauzes and silks, close-fitting underdresses like long coats, and graceful flowing robes.

Jewelry was not lacking either. Khadijah had silver anklets, and silver rings set with blue stones adorned her hands. She too had necklaces, though made of baser metal, set with coins made to simulate genuine ones. Nose rings, as well as earrings, were provided for her in this inexpensive costume jewelry, which was effective though cheap. She wore bracelets of heavy blue beads, as well as several silver ones.

The Henna Night was celebrated with the same enthusiasm as Fatima's, and the all-night party was participated in by all neighbors, relatives, and friends. The same deafening pounding on the drums in exciting rhythms, loud chanting, and frequent shrill trilling kept everyone's spirits keyed up to concert pitch all night long.

Next day, Khadijah was ceremoniously conveyed to her new home, with all her possessions—carried by cart, boat, or on the heads of porters and friends. The procession was accompanied by drums, and enlivened with clapping and trilling.

Rich or poor, the young wife was largely dependent in her future life on the disposition of her mother-in-law, who had it in her power to make the newcomer happy or miserable. Khadijah and Fatima were both marrying their cousins, but an uncle's wife was not necessarily kindly and congenial. Both brides would need to be docile and tactful in these new relationships.

The large family circles, with all the interplay of personalities, had a sociability and interest of their own.

Whatever the circumstances, no bride ever had a dull life.

III

Husbands and Wives

Fatima and her cousin Abdul Salaam were destined for each other from the time she was born. Among Moslem Arabs a paternal uncle's son is considered the inevitable husband for a girl unless there is some very strong reason against it. The usual term by which a wife refers to her husband—Ibn Ammi, "my paternal uncle's son"—demonstrates this. A mother's nephew is a good second choice, and failing that, anyone in the larger family circle.

This custom consolidates property and strengthens the bonds between families and tribes. Disregard of the general principle can lead to very serious results.

About ten years after Fatima's marriage Basrah society was rocked by an incident in high life, which fortunately had a happy ending. I dropped in to see Fatima one afternoon, and found a group of friends with her excitedly discussing the latest news over their tea glasses.

"What do you think!" she exclaimed to me after the exchange of greetings. "You know Amina Mansur."

Of course I did; she was the daughter of one of the leading families in the region and I knew them all well.

"She has always been intended for her cousin Bedr, from the time they were children. He went away to school, years ago, first to Egypt, and then to England. He's studying law at Oxford now, and we hear that he is having a *very* gay time.

"The family of Hajji Abdul Latif, do you know them?"

I did, slightly. They were good merchant stock, slightly *nouveau riche,* and certainly lower in the social scale than the great Mansur hierarchy.

"Well," continued Fatima with relish, "they thought that the Mansurs were not doing anything about getting Amina and Bedr married, and that maybe he had lost interest—they do, you know—or that something had gone wrong. She is getting quite old, too. They would *love* to have one of their sons marry into the Mansur family! And so they asked for Amina for Hajji Abdul Latif's son Ahmed.

"The Mansurs were so angry, you can't think. You know they are Sayyids [direct descendants of the Prophet]. They threatened to kill Ahmed and Hajji Abdul Latif, and Amina's father for even listening to the offer of marriage, and they have sent for Bedr to come home at once."

A chorus from the ladies gathered around the samovar discussed every aspect of this delectable piece of news with great gusto.

Next week I heard from Fatima's mother that peace was being made in the Mansur family circle. The head of the clan, a religious and scholarly old man who had retired to his country estates downriver, emerged from his seclusion and reconciled the angry factions. A large dinner was given by him at his town house, which was attended by all the men of the family.

Wedding preparations went briskly forward, and in due time the marriage was celebrated with all the festivities suitable for so auspicious an occasion.

Amina was a beautiful bride, and she and Bedr have had a happy and successful married life.

Another member of the Mansur family had a much more dramatic matrimonial experience. She had been informally earmarked from birth for a cousin—a half brother of Bedr's.

Again Fatima had exciting news to impart to me.

"Just listen to this! Nooria has always been intended for Mustafa Mansur. But his mother is a sister of Nooria's mother, and she has seen a lot of him all her life, especially when they were younger. Now she says he is very uninteresting to her, he seems like a brother, and she is going to marry his half brother Abdul Rizaq, who has just come back from England. He's been away for *years*. Isn't it exciting?"

I never did hear the inside story of how Nooria achieved this transition, which was against all precedent. She developed into a most poised and *soignée* young matron, and produced a large family of sons.

A good many years later when young women were beginning to have more freedom, though before they actually began to go unveiled in public, there were several "love matches" in Basrah circles. The girls and young men met, fortuitously, were attracted to one another, and then the families checked up to see if all was suitable. After that, the proceedings went forward in the orthodox manner.

Marriage is enjoined upon every Moslem, and celibacy was frequently condemned by Mohammed. It is related in the Traditions that the Prophet said, "When the servant of God marries, he perfects half of his religion." They also say, "On one occasion Mohammed asked a man if he was married, and being answered in the negative, he said, 'Art thou sound and healthy?' Upon the man's replying that he was, Mohammed said, 'Then thou art one of the brothers of the devil.'"

The Traditions are full of his quotations on the subject of marriage, and both the Koran and Traditions have many passages on the conditions of marriage.

Moslem men are permitted by the laws of Islam to marry four free wives, and to have as many slaves for concubines as they may have acquired. In the Koran, Surah: iv, 3, it states: "Of women who seem good in your eyes, marry two, or three, or four; and if ye still fear that ye shall not act equitably, then one only; or the slaves whom ye have acquired."

Marriage is forbidden between those who came within the prohibited degrees of kinship—consanguinity; or those closely related by alliance of affinity—in-laws. This includes a man's mother, sister, or daughter; paternal or maternal aunts; a father's wife (widowed or divorced); a daughter-in-law or sister-in-law; an uncle's wife or a brother's wife. Marriage is also prohibited between a man and his foster sister—one who has had the same "milk mother." This relationship is an old and honored one in the Arab world. If for any reason a mother is unable to provide milk for her own child and a foster mother is substituted, there is no feeling of rejection on the part of the child, but rather the addition of another close personal tie.

In general, the Koran allows a man to marry any woman who is not an idolatress, but a Moslem woman is permitted to marry only a believer.

Once the match has been approved by all concerned, there are long and intricate financial arrangements to be made. The prospective bridegroom, in addition to making a cash payment with which his betrothed provides her outfit and furniture, makes an agreement for another substantial payment to her in the event of his divorcing her. Should the wife divorce the husband, she must forfeit all her property bought with the cash payment, and in some cases also give an amount equal to the remainder of the settlement. When these arrangements are completed, the Mullah performs the actual ceremony. He must be in possession of a certificate from the religious courts, and he then proceeds to record the terms of the settlement. This becomes a legal document setting forth the details of the contract between the two parties. After this, the marriage takes place.

[35]

Polygamy is rapidly being discontinued in many Moslem countries, especially in the more progressive ones, in some cases even having been made illegal. The reasons for this are both social and economic.

However, at the time when I entered the Arab world, and for a good many years after, "partner wives" were a matter of course in all classes of society.

One primary reason, among rich and poor alike, was when wife number one had no children. In some cases she was lucky if she wasn't divorced, but merely had a partner wife brought in "on her head," as the saying went.

In agricultural villages, an extra wife was an economic asset and not a luxury. There were cows and chickens to be cared for, as well as the work in the date gardens. Seasonal crops were planted under the date trees and required careful cultivation.

In a large tribal village on the outskirts of Basrah, at the edge of the desert, the women all did porters' work. They specialized in carrying bricks and other building materials wherever construction work was going on. Two wives here were a distinct financial asset to a man.

Another reason was to consolidate family ties and keep property in the family. A man not only added to his prestige by having several wives, but he also had the benefit of an enlarged circle of relatives by affinity, which would increase the family strength and solidarity. Added to this was the advantage of providing for the surplus women—they outnumbered the men, and the system of polygamy assured them all security and status. In an era when the majority of women were illiterate, and most of those in the towns veiled and secluded, they needed a man to represent them in the courts when it was necessary, to see that they were given the rights laid down for them in religious law. A further basis for the system was the recognition of the fact that men were polygamous by nature, and that a legal and standardized provision for their physical needs was sensible and realistic. In both rich and poor households, a first wife who had reached middle age was often relieved to have her husband take a young wife. Often, as in the case of Fatima's father, wives lived apart and led completely detached lives.

In some of the great polygamous households each wife had her own suite of rooms and her own servants. In others which I knew, three or four wives lived together, the children were all brought up as one family, and on the surface at least there appeared to be harmony. Of course in many cases there was bitter rivalry and great unhappiness and jealousy.

One of my earliest pupils was married at about sixteen to a relative (not an own cousin), the only son of a prosperous grocer in another part of town. I often went to see Sabiha in her tall house, with its blue painted shutters, above the coppersmiths' bazaar, and became acquainted with her sharp-tongued and amusing mother-in-law. At the end of a year, Sabiha had not produced a baby and so it was decided that Hassan should take another wife. He married an own cousin this time. I never did know why he didn't marry her in the first place. She was an Ellawiya, or feminine Sayyid, a direct descendant of the Prophet and consequently someone very special. But she proved to have an even sharper tongue than her mother-in-law, and her pretty face concealed a bad-tempered and disagreeable personality. She quarreled with them all from the start—husband, his mother, and the poor little partner wife whom she despised and vilified on every occasion. The rows reached epic proportions, and were so noisy and vociferous that the neighbors complained to the head of the local religious courts. The Kadhi (the religious judge) had to take a hand, which was disgraceful for a family of such standing. Eventually she left and they were divorced. My little Sabiha kept her temper and held her tongue through all this uproar, placated her peppery mother-in-law, provided her young husband with a haven of rest, and was rewarded by Providence with a fine baby boy about a year after all the trouble.

Tribal sheikhs often married women from neighboring tribes because such connections consolidated their position and gave them valuable allies, as well as having financial benefits.

One of my closest friends over the years has been one of the wives of the late Sheikh Khazal of Mohammerah (now called Khoramshahr), who was the Sheikha of a small tribe in her own right. Her son, with four half brothers each of a different mother, was in my husband's boarding school in its earliest days. I used to visit her in her ancestral village up one of the tributaries of the Shatt-el-Arab River, and found the simple and dignified feudal existence a rich experience. Wearing Arab clothes, hearing no language but Arabic all day long, watching the small boats and larger river craft glide through the creeks among the date gardens; observing with fascination the domestic life in the great country household— it was all a pattern of living of which it was charming to be a part. One of her first gifts to me was a pair of slender gold bangles, slipped from her wrist to mine, which I have worn ever since.

She, and the other mothers, would send me huge pale blue glass jars of rose water from Persia; glazed pots of delectable date preserves flavored with ginger and sesame seeds; and sometimes the rather embarrassing present of live gazelles.

We used also to visit, with the boys, the Sheikh's huge sprawling palace on the big river where most of the wives had their establishments. Here all was bustle and activity, with constant goings and comings between the various groups. People arrived from Basrah, twenty miles up the river, or set out for a day in Mohammerah, a few miles to the south and up the River Karun. There were plans, news, gossip, shopping requests, and a thousand varied activities which kept the current of life at a lively flow.

[38]

The Sheikh had, besides his four legal wives, anything up to twenty other recognized semiofficial members in his harem. It always intrigued me that the chief wife, known as the Bibi Khanum (both words are Persian titles for a lady) held that position even though she was childless. She was deferred to not only by all the other women, but also by her noble husband himself. The first time we paid a visit to the main palace, Sheikh Khazal had just received a decoration from King George the Fifth of Great Britain. His little principality, nominally a vassal state within the Persian Empire, had treaty rights with Great Britain. (Whenever the British mail steamer passed his palace, on the way upriver to Basrah, it fired off a salute in his honor.) The Sheikh said to us when he was receiving us and his sons in his Durbar Room:

"I should like to show you my decoration from the English King, but the Bibi Khanum has it. She keeps all my valuables for me."

Sometimes it was difficult to be friendly with two wives if they were not on good terms. One of my first friends, whose son was in John's school, was bitterly jealous of a partner wife whom her husband married some years after I came to Basrah. He was a wealthy man and each wife had a handsome establishment, but it was quite clear that the second wife was his favorite. My friend made me feel that I was being disloyal to her if I had anything to do with number two. It was awkward for me, because I was constantly meeting the other wife at social affairs, she was always very cordial and friendly to me, and repeatedly invited me to come and see her.

Another delicate situation sometimes arose from the problem of which widow to condole with first, when a man died. Fortunately for me, I had been more or less adopted, at the beginning of my life in Basrah, by an old Hajjia whom I met through Fatima's family. One of her daughters eventually became my dearest Arab friend and has remained so to this day.

I could always ask them what was the proper thing to do in doubtful cases.

In the early decades of this century divorce was frequent and unpredictable in the Arab world. Early in my life in Basrah I was profoundly shaken by the first divorce I encountered of someone I knew well. My friend was an attractive and capable young woman, the mother of two nice children, a boy and a girl, and appeared to be cherished and appreciated by her husband's family. Her mother-in-law was in poor health and so Zeinab managed the establishment—kept the keys to the various storerooms, gave out supplies to the servants and supervised their work, and acted as hostess in the women's part of the house. As far as one could see, it was a happy and stable household.

One day, I went to see Fatima and found her unusually sober. After the salutations had been exchanged, I said, "Aren't you feeling well, Fatima?" She replied, "Not in my heart." Then she told me that Zeinab had been divorced and had gone off upcountry to her uncle's. I was stunned.

"But why?" I gasped.

"No one knows," answered Fatima sadly. She repeated what she had said to me on another occasion. "It is fate."

"Where are the children?" I inquired.

"Oh, they are here with their grandmother," answered Fatima.

The thing that horrified me most was that as far as I know, Zeinab never saw her children again. They were well and carefully brought up by the grandmother, went to school when the time came, and the boy, at least, sent away when older for further education in Egypt and Lebanon.

I used to inquire for her from mutual friends, but no one knew anything except that she had gone back to her uncle's village.

Years later, I heard from a friend that she was in Basrah with a husband. They had come for a few days on business.

I eagerly discovered where she was staying and got someone to take me there. It was an obscure and distant part of town and a very undistinguished house. Zeinab was so changed I would never have known her—a dour middle-aged woman with an expressionless face. She didn't seem especially pleased to see me and the visit was definitely not a success. I suppose it reminded her too forcibly of other days.

The Moslem law of divorce is founded on express injunctions in the Koran and also in the Traditions. There are large sections devoted to it in all works on Moslem jurisprudence. Briefly, the husband says "Thou art divorced" three times. After the first and second sentences he can change his mind, but it is irrevocable after the third sentence. The wife cannot then, under any circumstances, return to her first husband unless she has been married to another man and been divorced by him.

A husband may divorce his wife without any misbehavior on her part, or without assigning any cause.

A divorced woman usually returns to her father's house, or to an uncle. Her nearest relatives take her in as a matter of course. There are a few exceptions, dependent on varying circumstances.

The mother of one of my early pupils was divorced, but lived on contentedly in her former husband's large establishment. Her daughter had a half sister of about her own age, the two girls enjoyed being together, the other wife apparently had no objection, and they all lived together for years. My friend was an inoffensive soul and never made any trouble, kept to her own quarters and minded her own business. Occasionally the father of the girls would come in to speak to me when I was visiting them and their mothers, and I never got over the incongruity of seeing the divorced wife hastily veil her face when her former husband came into the room. Of course legally he was a strange man, and she was obliged to veil before him.

A friend of Fatima's and mine had a sad chapter in her early married life. She was a charming and high-spirited girl, an heiress whose father was dead and whose mother was a nonentity, and she was completely in the charge of her uncles. They arranged a good marriage for her with the son of a suitable family who were connections although not near relations. For a time all went well, Hassan and Fudhela really seemed to fall in love with each other, and were very happy. They had a most engaging curly-headed little girl who was the pet of the whole family circle.

Then I heard, again from Fatima, that Fudhela's uncles were making difficulties about property. It was all very involved, but evidently they made most outrageous demands and conditions to Hassan. He was high-spirited, too, and eventually was so exasperated that he said to them, in effect, "If you can't let my wife and me alone, and allow us to manage our own affairs, the situation will be impossible and I shall have to divorce her." To which they replied, in effect, "All right, divorce her!" and so he did.

I didn't know these facts until some years later—at the time, I just felt bad that such a nice couple couldn't manage to get along together.

Then one day, in great secrecy, Fudhela came to see me, with the curly-headed daughter who was by now quite a big girl. She told me that she had never stopped loving Hassan, that all the trouble was caused by her relatives, and that she would give anything to be married to him again. (We both knew that he had not married anyone else.) The little girl longed for her father and was always asking for him. Would I, could I, be a go-between? Well, this was a very delicate situation. I knew Hassan and his family well, but I also knew the whole rigid system of social proprieties. I assured her of my complete sympathy, and said I would think it over and see if there was anything I could do.

Accordingly I evolved a somewhat tortuous plan, using a

technique often employed in the Orient. I got my husband to send for a young man who was an intimate of Hassan's, with whom John had some perfectly legitimate business to transact, nothing whatever to do with the affair in which I was interested. I happened to meet this young man in the hall as he was going out, got him to come into my sitting room for a moment, and asked him if he would sound out his friend.

In due course I got a roundabout reply. The young man (Hassan) appreciated my concern and was deeply touched by it, but his honor was involved and it was impossible for him to make any sort of move toward reconciliation. I duly passed this message on to Fudhela. But I was not too downhearted; the first step had been taken. By this time I had learned thoroughly the truth of the saying "He who lives longest will see most."

I was absent from Basrah for some time after this, and on my return was delighted to hear that Hassan and Fudhela had remarried, and moved to Baghdad. He had received a substantial promotion in the government department in which he was employed, and I am sure they were both glad to go to another city and have a life of their own, well removed from her relatives.

Fatima was away, too, so I never did hear firsthand about the subsequent chain of events which led to this happy outcome.

However, I later asked an authority on Islamic law about it, and was assured that a formal contract of marriage with a third party could be arranged, which was legal and fulfilled all the requirements; the wife would then be divorced by the new husband, and would be free to marry her first mate. This was undoubtedly what had been done in Fudhela's case.

Permanent separations were common among the leading families. "We don't divorce, in the Family of the Mansur," I was told proudly in my early days. I had inquired about the status of a lady who had her own large establishment, but who obviously never had anything to do with her husband. This was partly in order not to disturb intricate financial arrangements and property holdings, and partly a matter of family pride.

In theory, a woman also has the right to divorce her husband for just cause. It is grounds for annulment of a marriage if she can prove before a Kadhi that he is not able to pay the dowry specified in the marriage contract, or provide her with necessities. In some Near East countries a Moslem woman can claim divorce from her husband if he breaks an agreement not to marry another wife, if he mistreats her, or if he absents himself from her beyond a specified period.

In actual fact, I only knew firsthand of one case where a woman instituted the divorce. Away back in the earliest days of my school, when we still took small boys into our kindergarten, I had as a pupil a little boy with a most attractive young mother who was a Mullaya, a religious reader. She was a widow when I first knew her, and her elderly husband had left her with a large property. Much of it was in real estate—houses in town, and date gardens—and she employed a young man to look after her business affairs. She had no male relatives near enough to act for her, which would have been the logical procedure, but they were all several hundred miles away. Not long after, we were all electrified to hear that she had married her agent. He was a presentable young man but not her social equal, and her friends disapproved of the match. Everyone predicted that it would not work out. They proved to be right, and in a year or two she tried to get him to divorce her. He refused flatly—whether because of her personal charms, or her bank account, or both, no one knew.

At all events, she was obliged to initiate proceedings herself, and as the complainant she had to fulfill the terms of their marriage contract and forfeit all her dowry and her outfit. She had beautiful Arab clothes and jewelry, and many were the oh's and ah's when it was known that she had handed them all over, as well as all the house furnishings, in addition to the substantial financial sums of the dowry.

The subject of marriage in Islam is inevitably associated with the veiling of women, and their seclusion in the harems. I early learned that the harem was the women's quarters, and that the *hareem* was the group of women who lived therein, whether many or few or only one. I have heard myself referred to as the "Hareem of Mr. Van Ess." Both these forms of the word come from the root meaning "forbidden" in Arabic.

Before the days of the Prophet Mohammed, the women of the desert dwellers went unveiled, and the women of the town covered their faces. In the tribe of the Prophet, the Koreish, veiling was the rule.

In an early revelation (Koran: xxxiii, 59 f) he commanded his own wives and daughters, and those of believers, to protect themselves by long veils when they went out in public. Later, he pronounced more definite rules regarding modest conduct and chastity (Koran: xxiv, 30 f), enjoining women not to display their charms to any men except their husbands, or persons so closely related to them as to come within prohibited degrees for marriage. Included in this were slaves (eunuchs particularly) and children too young to be conscious of difference of sex.

The harem system, and seclusion of women, is variously ascribed to influences from Persia, or to the rule of the Umayyid Caliphs of Damascus. At all events, by the time of the great Haroun al Rashid of Baghdad, a century and a half after the death of the Prophet, the system was fully established.

The veil was abolished in Turkey by Mustafa Kemal Ataturk, as part of the process of modernization, and in Persia by Shah Riza Pahlevi in 1936. In Iraq there has been no legislation, but the gradual disuse of the veil progressed unobtrusively.

"Just think, my friend," said Fatima to me one day when we had known each other for many years, and her own daugh-

ter was in school, "there are still places in other Arab countries where they won't let women use the telephone, for fear
a man might hear their voices; and they try to keep girls from
learning to write, because a man might see their handwriting!
I've heard that in one of their schools over yonder, they refused to let the girls study a certain textbook because it was
written by a man!"

"Did you ever hear, Fatima," I asked her, "that a woman's
footprints should not be seen by a man? And that is why they
allow their long robes to trail in the dust, so to obliterate
them?"

"It's possible!" she answered with energy. She glanced
down at her own neat buckled shoes and silk stockings, her
smart flannel dress which had been bought in a French shop
in Beirut the last time she went to Lebanon; then she patted
her freshly coiffured hair; and we looked at each other and
burst out laughing.

"Fatima," I said, "how do you like being called Abdul Salaam's Aqila?"

This was the common way to refer to a Moslem gentleman's
wife—if it was necessary to refer to her at all—and it is the
same word as the one used for a tethered camel.

"We-ll-ll," said Fatima thoughtfully, "I don't feel at all like
a camel. But you know"—brightening up—"they are using
Karina instead now, quite often. That means 'joined,' and at
least it means that the other person is joined, too!"

IV

Birth and Babies

Fatima had a son just before the first anniversary of her marriage. This was a most happy event, and all her family and friends rejoiced with her. When I went to see her and the baby, I found her room full of chattering friends and relatives. They were smoking and drinking tea and exclaiming loudly in praise to God. Fatima was propped up on pillows on her big bed, pale and pretty and looking suitably modest, but very proud. The baby was in an Arab cradle in the corner—a *karouk* as it is called—made of wood and swung from a large frame. This one had been in the family for years. His tiny face was bright red, he had a shock of dark hair, as most Arab babies do, and he had already been swaddled. As the years went by I became accustomed to seeing newborn babies dressed in all colors of the rainbow and their heads covered with little caps or scarves, but in my early days it looked very unbabyish to me and it was strange to see anything but white on a new baby.

"Ma sha' Allah!" I exclaimed when I saw Fatima's son. This is a pious ejaculation containing the name of God, and I added "May God keep him!"

I knew that one must never admire nor praise a baby, nor indeed any child, lest it attract the attention of the Evil Eye.

"Thank God for your safety!" I said to Fatima.

"Would you like to hold him?" asked Fatima's milk mother hospitably, after I had joined the group sitting on cushions against the wall.

I would like nothing better, so in a moment the little fellow was placed across my knees and I could examine him in detail. His little crimson face was crumpled in a huge yawn, and then he opened his eyes and fixed me with a baby stare. His eyes were large and black, and looked even larger because the lids had been rubbed with kohl—cooking-pot black—mixed with oil. This is supposed to make them strong.

"I put this on his navel, too, after I had tied off the cord with a woolen thread," the midwife informed me. She was sitting with the group, exuding satisfaction and happy to give full details about the whole process of the mother's labor and the child's birth.

I was inspecting the charms attached to the baby's swaddling clothes—blue buttons with seven eyes, cowries (shells), gallnuts, and triangular leather packets which I knew contained pieces of their holy script. I had already noticed similar charms attached to the top bar of his cradle, and saw that one of these dangling objects was a small gold box that contained a miniature Koran.

There was a dagger under the little mattress of his cradle, and his mother had a knife under her pillow.

"Did you have a hard time, Fatima?" I inquired presently, partly because it was expected of me, but mainly because I was really interested.

"She was splendid!" replied the midwife heartily, not giving the new mother a chance to reply except by a little grimace in my direction.

"I rubbed her abdomen with a knife, at the beginning, but praise be to God! the evil spirits did not trouble her. I had a piece of Keff Miriam in my bag and I put it in water where she could see it, and as it unfolded her pains were shortened, by the mercy of God!"

At that time I had no idea what Keff Miriam was, and wondered what connection there could be between Mary the Mother of Jesus, and Moslem childbirth.

Everyone present was delighted to enlighten me, and from the midwife, the milk mother, Fatima's own mother, and assorted aunts and in-laws, I soon heard all about it.

Keff Miriam means "Mary's palm" or hand, and is a small branchy growth known in English as rose of Sharon. It unfolds quickly in water, and most midwives carry a dried branch of it in their bags. The legend is that the Virgin Mary held on to the tree which produces this growth, when she was in labor, and was immediately delivered of the Christ Child.

Since then, I have seen dried Keff Miriam strung up in bazaars all over the Near East, and realize how universal its use is when women are undergoing the pains of childbirth.

"I had a Mullaya ready," went on the midwife chattily, "to place a Koran on Fatima's head and open the pages one by one, and then to read Sura Miriam, if she needed any more help."

"That is the chapter about Mary the Mother of Jesus, in your book, isn't it?" I ventured.

"Yes indeed!" put in one of the aunts. She was an amateur Koran reader herself, and was delighted that I knew about it.

"It tells us how the Prophet Isa, upon him be peace, was born under a palm tree, and how in his cradle he testified to his mother's innocence and to his own mission."

I knew that Isa was the Moslem name for Jesus, and that they always referred to him as a prophet.

"What did you do with the placenta?" asked one of the visitors in an aside to the midwife. She used the term "the sister" which had to be explained to me, as hitherto I had only heard the placenta referred to as the "female neighbor."

"It was thrown into the river," replied the midwife crisply. "Running water is much the best."

Then I heard a low-toned colloquy of how, in one case, where a mother had previously lost several children in infancy, the afterbirth was sprinkled with aloes and placed in a jar which was sealed with mud and then hung on a palm tree.

"In Bahrain," volunteered a traveled member of the group, "they bury the placenta with salt sprinkled over it, to appease the jinn, in the earth. Arabs there bury it face up [cord side down] so the woman may have more babies."

"Have you carried him upstairs yet?" asked a hitherto silent visitor.

"Of course!" spoke up Fatima's milk mother. "*I* carried him up to the roof as soon as he was washed and dressed."

"When are you going to take him on the Dowra?" inquired the same lady, this time of the midwife. "Very soon now," was the answer.

This was something new to me, so I inquired with interest what the Dowra was and received a perfect chorus of answers, contributed by every member of the group.

The Dowra is a perambulation, literally a "going around," when the baby is taken to visit all the places which might otherwise cause him harm, unless respectfully recognized.

"I shall put a copy of the Verse of the Throne on his chest, and a rag with Seven Odors," the midwife stated. This verse, the famous Ayat-al-Kursi, is the favorite passage from the Koran to protect against spells and demons. It goes:

God! There is no God but He: the Living, the Abiding. Neither slumber seizeth Him, nor sleep. To Him belongeth whatsoever is in earth. Who is he that can intercede with Him but by His own permission? He knoweth what hath been before them, and what shall be after them; yet nought of His knowledge do they comprehend, save what He willeth. His THRONE reacheth over the heavens and the earth, and the upholding of both burdeneth Him not: and He is the High, the Great.

"I shall have a knife, myself," continued the midwife, "and some rolls of writing against evil spirits."

"Where do you carry him, here in Basrah?" asked a lady who lived in Baghdad and was down on her first visit.

"To at least seven places of public gathering, and more if possible," was the reply.

"To a mosque, a synagogue, and a church; the bazaars, the dyers' vats, the slaughterhouse; and as many bridges as possible. One must cross the bridges, too."

"Don't forget, at the dyers' vats," put in Fatima's milk mother, "to dip your fingers in seven colors, and to dab a little of the blue on the baby's forehead."

"In Baghdad," said the visiting lady, "we carry babies to the Street of the Makers of Red Slippers, and also to the Tōp Abu Hezama."

"And what is that?" we all asked.

"A very ancient cannon, with magic powers," she informed us importantly. "In the old days it was decorated with votive rags, and people used to pass newborn babies around it, and put their heads in the muzzle!"

By now it was time for this particular baby to be handed up to his mother for sustenance.

"I hope he wet on your lap," said the midwife kindly to me as she lifted him up. "It would be a sign that you would soon become pregnant."

When I next visited Fatima, some weeks later, she was by herself (for a wonder) and we had a chance for a much more confidential talk.

"How lucky I was!" she remarked to me, casting a proud maternal glance toward the doll-like figure in the cradle.

"Mohammed came along very quickly, and I didn't need to have any disagreeable things done to me. My cousin had very slow pains, and do you know what her midwife did? She boiled an onion and took off the outside skin, and then put it, while it was hot, up inside the poor girl—where the baby's head was. She said it hurt terribly. Even then, it was a long time before the baby was born, and she was quite badly torn. They mixed some kind of medicine called anza root with a cock that had been roasted whole—feathers and all!—and put it on to heal her."

"Has Mohammed's cord dropped off yet?" I asked, after we had discussed the unpleasant medications to which Fatima's cousin had been subjected.

"Oh yes, some time ago!" she said gaily. "And do you know where we threw it? Into the courtyard of the mosque, where the Mullah sits with his pupils. So that he will be a clever scholar when he grows up!"

"Why not outside his father's office, so that he'll be a good businessman?" I asked, to tease her.

"That would have been quite possible too," was the serious reply. "And when I have a daughter, I'll bury her cord in the house, so she will grow up fond of domestic duties!

"You haven't been to the bazaar today, have you?" Fatima asked me abruptly.

"No, I came straight from home," I said in surprise. "Why?"

"You probably don't know, but it is said to be very dangerous to a baby if someone comes in with a purchase she has just made," she explained in a relieved way.

I had known that one ought never to wear perfume when going to see a newborn baby, as all smells are supposed to have an effect, and "effluvium" is a very delicate subject. However, this about bazaar purchases was new to me, and I asked for further details.

"Well, a woman came in to a house down the street, not thinking about the baby there. She had a piece of red cloth in her basket, and also some tomatoes. The baby turned red!" Fatima assured me solemnly. "And it had convulsions!

"In one of the villages in our date gardens, a man came into a hut with a lemon he had just bought. Not long after, the baby became yellow, and had a very bad case of jaundice. Fortunately there was a wise midwife there who knew just what to do. She went to my aunt's house and borrowed a long gold necklace, long enough to put the baby through, and then draped the gold coins attached to the necklace over its hands. It got well!" she concluded triumphantly.

Just for good measure, she added a bit about another color. "You know how lucky blue is?" she asked me. "Turquoises, or seven-eye beads, or even just pieces of a broken blue-glazed pot. If a baby turns blue, or is blue at birth as they sometimes are, something blue must be attached to his clothing."

On another visit we discussed names. I had several little girls in my school called Om el Khair—the Mother of Good— and so many Fatimas and Khadijahs that I had to number them. Fatima was the Prophet Mohammed's daughter, and Khadijah his first wife.

"They are two of the four women who the Prophet, upon him be peace, said were perfect," my Fatima informed me. "The others are the Virgin Mary and Asiyah, the wife of Pharaoh."

I had a number of little Miriams in my school, too—the form of the name always used in Arabic for Mary.

The group around the samovar laughed when I told them the names of some of my village pupils. Garbage, Dogs, Angry, She-doesn't-belong-to-us, and Daughter of the Air had astonished me until I realized that mothers chose these for their children in the hope that the powers of evil would be deceived and think that the bearers of such derogatory names could not be worth the attention of a malignant fate.

"Have you anyone named Enough?" asked Fatima mischievously. "A child is sometimes called that when the mother doesn't want any more!"

They then explained to me why an attractive baby I had seen at a well-to-do neighbor's was dressed in clothes entirely made from small patches of different kinds of cloth.

"All her babies died!" said Fatima sadly. "So she vowed that she wouldn't buy any clothes for this one for a whole year—she would beg pieces of cloth from her friends."

At the same house I had seen a chubby toddler with long curls, earrings and tiny bracelets set with turquoises, and I addressed it in the feminine. Everyone laughed, and the grandmother said, "It is a little boy!"

The mother had vowed she would dress him in girls' clothes for several years, lest the fact that she had a son might attract the envy of evil powers.

After the birth of her first child, a mother is almost invariably known as Mother of So-and-So. I had been called Om John for many years before I learned that there is a technical anthropological term for the parent deriving a name from the child, and that "teknonymy" was the word for this usage which was so familiar to me in practice. The father also sometimes shares this nomenclature. My husband was often addressed by his intimates as Abu John—the Father of John.

Childless women are often called Om Isa or Om Hussein— Isa being Jesus, and Hussein the grandson of the Prophet Mohammed.

A very few outstanding women continued to be called by their own names, preceded by the title which indicated their importance, even after they had children. Mullaya Medina and Mullaya Kadhimiyah were great religious leaders and teachers and were two of the outstanding figures in my early days in Basrah. Another was Ellawiya Zenoba, a feminine Sayyid who was a direct descendant of the Prophet. Several Hajjias, women who had made the pilgrimage to Mecca, were known by this title, followed by their personal names.

The same was true of some of the leading midwives. A midwife is a Jidda—the same word as "grandmother." The Red Sea port of Jidda contains the reputed tomb of Eve, the "Grandmother of all Living," and hence received its name.

Fatima's midwife was Jidda Atiya. We were drawn to each

other first because we had the same Arabic name. Atiyat-Allah means the Gift of God, and is the direct translation of my Christian name, Dorothy, so I was called that by my Arab friends until I earned the more honorable title of Om John.

From Jidda Atiya I learned first of many of the practices employed in the hope of inducing pregnancy.

My friend Fatima was not only lucky in having an easy time in labor and delivery, but still more fortunate in producing a baby with reasonable promptness after her marriage.

Brides are watched closely by all the women of the family, and if they do not show signs of pregnancy within the first few months, measures are resorted to, increasing in number and complexity as time goes on. If it becomes a matter of years, and a woman fears she may be barren, the situation is still more urgent.

"My dear Atiya," began the midwife to me one afternoon when we were settled in her little room for a good long talk, and she was puffing away at the water pipe to which she was addicted, "a pilgrimage is the first thing! If Fatima had not conceived readily—God be praised! I should have advised the family to take her to Baghdad, and have her spend the night at the shrine of Abdul Qadir al Gailani, in the great Gailani Mosque. That is a very powerful place."

"I've heard of a Christian shrine in Baghdad, too," said I, "where Moslem women sometimes go. Do you know about that?"

"Certainly!" replied the Jidda emphatically. "That is the ancient Armenian Church of St. Miskinta, and a barren woman must stay there overnight, with an iron collar fastened around her neck. If it becomes undone by itself, it is a sign she will surely have a child."

"Do you know anyone who did?" I asked somewhat skeptically.

"So they say, so they say!" she murmured, with another pull at her water pipe.

[55]

"Then there is the tomb of Sheikh Zuwair," she continued, "where a woman takes dust from the tomb, mixes it with water, and drinks it. My husband's niece went to a tomb in the desert outside Baghdad—the shrine of Junaid, a great Mystic—and water from a well on the enclosure was poured over her, three times."

By this time a neighbor had joined us, and had contributions to offer to our symposium.

"You know the tomb of Bahlul?" she asked, and Jidda Atiya nodded vigorously.

"Well, my neighbor's daughter went up there, she had been married five years, and never a sign of a baby, poor thing! She made a little hut of palm fronds and placed it in front of the tomb, and tied together a few rags to put in it, to resemble a child—just to remind the saint that she had made her vow. Of course she gave the Sayyid in charge of the tomb a very generous gift. *And*"—impressively—"in less than a year she had a beautiful little son! And after that, a girl—nice to have a daughter, if you've had a boy first."

We all agreed that this was a pilgrimage that paid handsome dividends.

"What did she vow, at the saint's tomb?" I inquired curiously. I had seen the baby in patches, and the boy dressed like a girl, and I wondered what other sorts of vows were popular.

"Oh, she vowed that if she had a son, she would find a poor woman who had borne a boy the same day, and clothe him and provide for him while he was small, and have him circumcised at the same time as her own."

"Did she do it?" we asked, as this seemed rather a large commitment.

"Indeed she did!" was the answer. "It would be *very* bad luck not to fulfill a vow. She got him a nice little date-stick cradle, and a red quilt; clothes, and a cap with blue beads just like her own baby's. And when they began to creep—fortunately at about the same time—she got them both *khilkhal* for their ankles."

I had seen and admired these charming little anklets, set about with tiny bells, worn by nearly all babies. They were of gold, silver, or white metal, according to the means of the parents. The idea was that wherever the creeper or toddler got to, the mother could locate him by the tinkle of the bells.

I had noticed small flags fluttering all over the tombs of local saints, up and down the roads along the river, and out on the desert.

"Are those all put there by women who want children?" I asked my friends. "And do they all make vows?"

The answer was "yes" to both questions.

"Some of the vows are for small deeds of charity," explained Jidda Atiya. "A poor woman can't do very much. Often they promise to feed a beggar every night in the fasting month of Ramadhan. Or maybe they will prepare a tray of henna and myrtle for the next wedding among their acquaintances. Sometimes a woman promises to do some extra fasting, after the fasting month is finished. This is pleasing to God."

At another session, after I knew her more intimately, the Jidda confided to me some of the other methods employed in hope of making a barren woman fruitful. Many of them were connected with corpses, tombs, shrines, and graveyards.

"A barren woman should gaze on the face of a corpse, preferably another woman," she stated in oracular tones. "A Moslem woman goes to the Jewish cemetery and jumps over seven graves. Of course the Jewish woman who is barren goes to the Moslem cemetery. Or the childless woman takes a rag she has used at her 'time of the month' and throws it between the cemeteries of two different sects, not her own. Then she pollutes the graves, whispering over each one what she has done.

"I've heard," she continued, warming to her subject, "that in Baghdad a woman sometimes takes the rag from her time of the month and drops it on the threshold of a house during the night, then knocks loudly, covers her face, and runs away before the door is opened.

"In Amarah," she went on, "a Moslem woman who fears that her barrenness may be due to some sudden happening that was of ill omen to her, goes at night to a house in the Jewish quarter and relieves herself on the threshold of some house. Then she holds her garment with one hand and knocks on the door with the other. When the people of the house call out 'Who is there?' she doesn't answer, but escapes."

By far the most unpleasant remedy suggested for a bride who is not immediately fertile, was confided to me long afterward. If she has previously met another bride at the public bath, who she hears is lucky enough to be pregnant, she must seek her out with an amazing request. She asks the fertile bride to secure some of her husband's urine, or the urine of both, and for seven weeks after this, at her weekly visit to the bath, she gets a friend to pour a little of it over her head when she is not expecting it. At the same time a little rhyme is repeated. If this is not efficacious she sends word to know if she may crawl through the straddled legs of the pregnant woman's husband. (This would be quite a feat, since she would be wrapped in her abba, with a tightly drawn veil across her face.)

Fatima had one cousin of whom she was very fond, who never did have any children. The poor girl was dragged all over the country on pilgrimages, was taken to every doctor and quack that her family heard of, and tried every midwife's suggested remedies. They listened to all the lore on the subject from every source. Fatima's comment to me, which I had heard her make before on other subjects, was a sober "It is Fate."

There was a time-honored Moslem procedure after the birth of every baby. When the midwife cut the cord, she asked, "What is the name of this child?" and no matter what they intended to name it eventually, the answer must be Mohammed for a boy, and Fatima or Miriam for a girl.

Then the baby must be washed all over (cleanliness is from Allah and dirt from the devil) and bound in swaddling clothes. A large triangular piece of cloth was used, and the baby was laid on it with the point down. Both arms were wrapped around—usually parallel to the body, though in some circles they were crossed over the chest. Swaddling was continued four to six months, often using a "half swaddle" which left the arms free, after two or three months. The swaddling cloths were changed as often as necessary, and some mothers used a rubber tube reaching from inside the cloths down through them and then through the cradle to a receptacle placed beneath.

When the newborn child was clean and swaddled, if it was a boy he would then be carried to an assembly of male relatives and friends. Here someone qualified would recite the Azan, the Summons to Prayer, in the infant's right ear, and then another longer one called Iqamah, the Standing, in his left ear. This custom was founded on the example of the Prophet, of whom it was related that he did this at the birth of his grandson Hassan. A girl baby had the Azan and Iqamah read in her ears by the grandmother or a respected aunt, or other relative, but it could be done by the midwife, especially if the infant was not healthy. This ceremony being over, alms were distributed and Fatihas recited for the health and prosperity of the child.

The Fatiha, literally an opening, is the first chapter of the Koran, the Chapter of Praise. It is greatly venerated and used on all occasions, and is in general the equivalent of the Lord's Prayer among Christians.

In the Name of God, the Compassionate, the Merciful
Praise be to God, Lord of the Worlds,
The compassionate, the merciful.

King on the day of reckoning.
Thee only do we worship, and to Thee do we cry for help.
Guide Thou us on the straight path,
The path of those to whom Thou hast been gracious,
With whom Thou are not angry, and who go not astray.

According to the Traditions, the amount of silver given in alms should be of the same weight as the hair on the infant's head, the child's hair being shaved for this purpose.

Tradition appoints the seventh day for the naming of the child, and a ceremony called the Aqiqah when two sheep are sacrificed if the baby is a boy. (Only one for a girl!)

The mother is purified ceremonially on the fortieth day by an official visit to the bath, and resumes her normal life. In olden times, this was the day when the baby was first placed in the swinging cradle.

"You know," said Fatima to me, "as soon as Mohammed can talk, I must teach him the Fatiha, or at least by the time he is four years, four months, and four days old!

"Think of that little scrap saying 'In the Name of God, the Compassionate, the Merciful'!

"After that," she said with a sigh, "I suppose he will have to go to school, to learn his letters and to read the Koran! He will go to the Mullah in the courtyard of the mosque near here."

The next great event in the little boy's life was his circumcision, when he was about seven years old. This ancient custom, dating from the time of Abraham, was universal among Moslems. Although, curiously enough, it is nowhere mentioned in the Koran, it is based on the teaching and practice of the Prophet.

It was certainly a gala day. In the forenoon, Mohammed was dressed in gay and elegant clothes, with a sort of turban-like arrangement on his head, and paraded through the streets in his neighborhood riding a richly caparisoned horse. Behind him on the same horse was one of his pals from a village on the family estates down the river. A second horse, not quite so handsomely equipped, followed with two more little boys who were fellow pupils with Mohammed in the Koran school. The horses were led, and men carrying silk handkerchiefs walked beside them, flapping the flies away from the children's faces. A local band walked at the head of the procession, keeping up ear-splitting music throughout the tour. Several flags from the mosque were carried along, to attract the eye and to distract attention from the child. I was assured that this was a precaution against the much-dreaded "evil eye."

A group of us women were interested observers from the veranda of the inside courtyard at Fatima's house. The barber who was to perform the operation was waiting in a lower room, with his rather primitive instruments (scissors, a razor, and bamboo forceps) laid out on a white-covered table.

When the procession came into the courtyard, the four little boys were hoisted down from their horses and whisked into the barber's room. The band took their stand outside the door and continued to play even louder than before.

"Why do they keep on playing?" I whispered over the din to Jidda Atiya, who was next to me, her veil drawn tightly across her face.

"So that if the children cry, they will not be heard!" was what seemed to me a rather callous reply.

However, the operation was soon over and there seemed to be no ill effects. The little boys lay down on specially prepared beds and were plied with food and drink and sweetmeats, and made a great fuss over, all day.

That night, Fatima and her mother-in-law and all the women of the family connection gave a huge party for all their friends. The guests wore their most colorful outfits and their gorgeous Arab jewelry, and the courtyard was spread with rugs and blazing with lights. Negro women with drums played and sang; and several Mullayas took part in the religious readings, thanking God for Mohammed's safety and well-being. At midnight a lavish supper was served, and the festivities went on all night, as they had on Fatima's Henna Night at the time of her marriage. As on that occasion, and on many others, I excused myself before the dawn prayer call, but was followed with protests for not seeing the party through.

The time when a boy or girl completes the reading of the Koran is often the occasion for celebrations. After this, there are no special landmarks in a child's life.

Fifteen years is set as the age when manhood or womanhood is attained, and may be earlier if there are definite signs of physical maturity.

Arabs are very fond of children, and every man's keenest desire is to have sons. Girls are petted and cherished, however, especially if they come after boys in the family. The Prophet reproved his people for lamenting the birth of a daughter, although a girl's inheritance is only half a portion, and in a law court it requires the testimony of two women to rebut that of one man.

When my second child was born, all my friends rejoiced with me because they knew how greatly I wanted a daughter.

She was only a few weeks old, when one morning I was called into the living room and told that Abdul Lutif Pasha el Mendil wanted to pay his respects to me. He was a good friend of my husband's, and belonged to one of the leading families of Basrah. Somewhat mystified, I went in and received him. In the most courtly manner he said to me, after exchange of the customary salutations:

"I know from my family how earnestly you desired a daughter, and I wish to give you my congratulations because God has granted your wish."

Then he went on in sonorous phrases, of which only the incomparably beautiful Arabic language is capable, to wish the child health, long life, and every blessing. He gracefully included me, and at the end made a tactful reference to my husband and my son.

As he left, he put a small parcel into my hand. We exchanged the ceremonious expressions of farewell, and when he had gone I opened his gift. It proved to be a lovely gray and white silk abba delicately embroidered in gold thread.

In later years he became a member of the Cabinet of King Feisal the First, and as much as the abba, I still cherish a picture of him with the then Prime Minister and his brother.

The Traditions have long dissertations on the training of children. So does the famous Moslem scholar of the eleventh century, al-Ghazali, whose great work *The Revival of the Sciences of Religion* contains a special section on methods for the education of boys and the improvement of their moral character. Nothing was said about girls! It was generally considered by the old writers to be inadvisable to teach girls to read and write, and the Prophet was often quoted as saying: "Do not let them frequent the roofs; do not teach them the art of writing; teach them spinning and the chapter of the Koran called En Nur [The Light]."

On the whole the Arabs have a tendency to spoil their sons, preferring to give them the pleasure of immediate indulgence rather than the long-range benefit of discipline. They are relieved when they can turn over to a school the less agreeable aspects of child training which form character.

However, Arabs of the old school placed great stress on respect to elders, to teachers, and to other learned and venerable persons. This was particularly noticeable among people with any Turkish background, but it was equally true of the families with long traditions of honorable conduct. Grown-up sons would never smoke in the presence of their fathers, at least in public. A former pupil of mine had a successful career as a teacher, but for years after she was on terms of

equality with me professionally, she could never bring herself to light a cigarette in my presence.

The sons and grandson of the late Sheikh Khazal of
Mohammerah, whom I have mentioned previously, loved and
venerated my husband, and never forgot the years when he
was educating them and training their characters. Nor do they
forget that I once "mothered" them in the boarding school,
and though some of them are now more than middle-aged,
whenever they meet me after an absence they kiss my hand.
I have had this happen to me in front of a crowded open
coffee shop at a busy corner of the bazaar, and at a cocktail
party, and I find it deeply moving, and only slightly embarrassing.

V

Blood Is Thicker Than Water

The family is the basis of society in Iraq, and its solidarity and responsibility goes back much farther than the coming of Islam to the country thirteen centuries ago. Kinship through the male line establishes lineage, and the tribes, with their subsections and sections and confederations, all have strong traditions concerning their founding ancestor. The pattern is by no means confined to the desert tribes, but extends through the agricultural population and the people of the villages and of the towns, as they all share in the deep-rooted traditions of the past. There are ideals of behavior that stem from their common origin, which give them unity and mutual understanding.

The immediate family—the man and his wife and children—is closely bound to the extended family, which is the nucleus of social organization. This consists of three generations who trace descent in the male line, and includes paternal grandparents, married sons and their wives, the sons' married and unmarried sons, and unmarried daughters. It may include widowed or orphaned female relatives of the senior male, in whom authority is usually vested. By tradition, marriage

[65]

should be confined to this lineage. The bonds of the nuclear family are close, but they exist within the framework of the extended family, whose interests always come first. A group of several lineages, or subtribes, may have rivalries or feuds among themselves, but if they are threatened from without the ranks close, and without hesitation they make common cause. Identification with this closely knit group gives a sense of security and confidence to every member.

The economic role of the family, and its interdependence in business or public life, is just as strong as in domestic affairs and personal relationships. Relatives are expected to help each other in getting jobs and in gaining favorable consideration in any situation. In a country where almost the only form of social security is the family system, it is taken for granted that the person who has a job shall support the members of the family who are unable to work, or who are unemployed. It was estimated a few years ago that every person in employment had at least four dependents. Working members of a household pool their resources, and accept without question the fact that the claims of the family come before those of the individual. Children are an economic asset among the poor, and boys (and sometimes girls) often begin to contribute to the family income at an early age. In country areas, branches of the extended family are usually closely associated in their economic activity, working the land together, with traditional reciprocal relationships and mutual obligations and benefits.

An important social institution among the nomads, and to some extent with the settled population, is the Khamsah— the group of five. This includes all a man's patrilinear relatives who are within five degrees of relationship, and they are the traditional group who are responsible for the honor and prestige of the tribe. It is incumbent on each one of them to take his part when necessary in affairs of honor: avenging the death of a fellow tribesman; "washing out the stain" if a woman's good name is involved; and in general being at all times ready to give his allegiance to tribal concerns. This loyalty always comes first.

Traditions of hospitality are likewise strong. Guests, to any of the desert tribes, are always entitled to shelter, protection, and food, with no questions asked—as to name, errand or destination—for three days. Usually the information is volunteered before that time. Anyone in danger may seek protection by uttering the word "Dachil"—the equivalent to "I seek refuge"—and then it is incumbent on the whole tribe to guard his safety. The sheikh, who is the head of the tribe, enjoys all the dignity and prerogatives of his position, but is always accessible to the humblest member.

All the great landowning families in the fertile river section of lower Iraq have large country houses on their estates as well as residences in town. These are used for entertaining, and are often occupied by branches of the family with a taste for rural life, or by the member of the clan who is directly responsible for the management of the estate.

The *fellahs*—farmers—who live and work on these estates, in villages or in scattered settlements, have a hereditary and somewhat feudal relationship with their landlords and proprietors, and feel a definite sense of identification with the clan or family.

When Sheikh Chassib, the oldest son of the late Sheikh Khazal of Mohammerah, in Arabistan, died in 1949, the family had been broken up for years. Some of them were in exile; the old sheikh himself had died in Teheran. But when the body of Sheikh Chassib was brought back to Iraq for burial, thousands of villagers and countryfolk from former Khazal estates all over the region gathered to march through the streets of Basrah behind the coffin, chanting and wailing and lamenting in the traditional manner.

The same thing happened at the funeral of Sheikh Salih Bashayan, a former President of the Iraq Senate, and the representative for his country at the League of Nations in Geneva, when Iraq became a member of that organization. When he died, his body was brought by plane from Baghdad to Basrah, to be buried in the family cemetery in the Mishraq Mosque, on the outskirts of Basrah. It was followed the whole long way, on foot, by a large gathering of people who were connected with the Bashayan estates. As they marched they chanted mournfully, "We have lost our Protector and Governor."

Dependents, both in households and on the land, usually receive new clothes from their patrons at each major Moslem holiday, and a bag of rice each season, likewise a tin of *dihn*—cooking fat. Marriages are arranged or assisted, and advice and help are expected and received in all the crises of life. Many of the household retainers in southern Iraq are former African slaves or their descendants. They mix and intermarry freely with the Arab population and there is little, if any, color prejudice.

Some of these Negro women, who are called *waseefas*, have strong and assertive personalities. Fatima told me an entertaining incident about one of them who went with "her" family to Baghdad, when the Arab gentleman to whose household she belonged was a deputy to the Iraq Parliament. There are very few Negroes in Baghdad, so she was something of a curiosity, and she was annoyed at having street urchins run after her when she was out of doors, jeering at her and calling "Ya Sambo!" She complained to her master, and he suggested that instead of going unveiled, as Negro women usually do in Basrah, and wearing the coarse homespun wool abba of the lower classes, she be provided with the type of abba worn by ladies of the gentry, and a veil to cover her face, when she went out in Baghdad.

"Then no one will know but what you are my mother!" he said jokingly.

"Oh, no!" she protested. "It isn't *that* bad. I'll curse, and I'll beat them up, and I'll manage for myself!"

The custom of intermarrying within the extended family group results in the most complicated system of relationships, and a complete confusion of the different generations. I soon found out that a knowledge of how it all fitted together was indispensable if I wanted to understand the people of the land.

"Who is that pretty little girl over there, Fatima?" I asked her one day when I was at her mother's, and there were several groups in the large reception room.

"Which one?" looking around. "Oh, that's my aunt."

"Your aunt!" I exclaimed. "She looks only half your age!"

Fatima laughed. "So she is! My grandfather married a young wife when he was quite old, and he has several children younger than my brothers and me. They live down at Abul Khassib now."

Fatima's aunts and cousins from Abul Khassib, about eight miles away, were always going to and fro, and she often went down to the pleasant country town spread out along the creeks among the date gardens.

Another day I was crossing the schoolyard during the noon recess and saw one of our young sheikhs, from a desert tribe, waiting outside the door of the primary school.

"Aren't you going in to have your lunch, Khalid?" I asked him, for I could see the boys in the dining room of the boarding school beginning their meal.

"I have to wait for my uncle," he said, and just then a very small boy emerged from the school and gave some of his stack of books to his very large nephew to carry.

Again I was surprised, and Khalid told me that the child belonged to a late-married young wife of his grandfather, and had been entrusted to his special care when he came away to school.

The Arabs, when I first came to know them, had little or

[69]

no home life in the sense in which we understand it. Fatima's husband had a comfortable *mejliss*—literally a "sitting place" —in connection with his office, which was in a building adjoining the house. Here he spent his leisure, except for meals, and even those would often be sent in to him there on a huge round tray. Here he entertained his friends and received his visitors.

All large dwellings, in both town and country, had what amounted to a separate smaller house, called the *diwan*, for the men of the family, with a door leading from its court-yard into the women's part of the house—the harem.

Men of the middle and lower classes frequented the coffee shops, where they could meet their friends for business and pleasure, and hear the news. A few generations ago this would have been by word of mouth, or by listening to some-one reading aloud from a newspaper; later of course the radio gave them continuous broadcasts, and every coffee shop had one, turned up as high as possible all the time.

They would sip endless glasses of sweet tea or small cups of coffee, and smoke cigarettes or tiny Arab pipes or the ever-popular water pipe. The name of this was the *nargileh*, but it was familiarly known as the "hubble-bubble," descriptive of the sound made as the smoker drew on the pipe which led through the water. Old ladies often affected this, too, and I had one friend who took a little black slave girl with her everywhere, to carry the complicated and bulky apparatus and to light the charcoal in the tiny cuplike brazier at the top where the tobacco was burned.

But even though on the everyday plane men and women lived their lives apart, family solidarity was the basis of so-ciety, and when anything happened that touched their honor or their safety, the ranks closed.

I was greatly shaken when the first "honor killing" oc-curred of someone whom I knew. A girl of good family had either gone astray, or been accused of it so publicly that her good name was gone forever, and her father killed her. From the Arab point of view it was completely justifiable—in fact, obligatory—although it was in violation of modern criminal law. This is called "the washing away of the disgrace." Eventually the father was pardoned, and resumed his normal place in society—if anything with enhanced prestige.

Another girl whom Fatima and I both knew well got herself talked about by being accused of sending notes by her little brother to a young man. Whether there was any truth in the accusation I never knew, but she was cold-shouldered socially, and never was considered eligible for marriage. She became that extremely rare creature in Moslem society, an old maid.

Fatima had a harrowing tale told her by a friend who had been in a neighboring country, of a girl there whose father had walled her up in a room in the family house. A brick wall was built up in front of the cell where she was imprisoned, with an opening above the level of her head when she was standing up, through which food and drink were passed to her.

"I'd rather be killed outright!" exclaimed Fatima with a shudder.

Eventually, after some months, the friend had reported that the girl was let out—whether because her innocence was proved, or because of the intervention of friends, Fatima didn't know.

The most celebrated affair of honor I ever knew stirred all Iraq when it happened. It was after the establishment of the Kingdom of Iraq, and Baghdad society had become, on the surface, much more modern and progressive than it had been even a short time before.

The Minister of Interior was a gifted young man whose father's early life had been a success story. From humble beginnings, he had achieved a prosperous and honorable career.

The father was dead, but the son was a worthy successor and everyone thought highly of him.

He wanted to marry the daughter of one of the members of a proud and ancient family, who was living at the time with her widowed mother in Syria. It was said that he asked advice before he took the final step, fearing that he would not be considered the young woman's equal by her family, but was assured by his friends that Iraq was now an advanced, up-to-date country and that old prejudices were dying out. He went to Syria and married the girl quietly, with her mother's consent, and he brought her back to Baghdad.

Not long after, the ranking member of the tribe to which the bride's family belonged walked into the government building where the Cabinet offices were, went in to the Minister of the Interior, and pronouncing the one word "Traitor!" shot him dead. The Sheikh then stepped out into the corridor, told the astonished guards what he had done, and gave himself up.

He was a quiet, dignified man who lived very simply in his desert encampment. He had no personal animosity whatever against the man whom he killed, but as the head of the confederated tribes to whom the young wife's family belonged, it was his duty to wipe out the stain on their honor, caused by one of their number marrying a person of inferior birth.

The most poignant part, to me, was a message the Sheikh sent to my husband from prison. His two boys were in our boarding school, and he said, "Tell Mr. Van Ess that my sons are now his sons, that whether I live or die, I commit them to him as a sacred trust."

He was first sentenced to be executed. Then it was changed to life imprisonment—then to fifteen years—and later to seven. As I recall, he was actually released in about two and a half years.

After his release, the Sheikh had a tremendous welcome when he returned to Basrah by train, on his way back to his home in the desert. All his retainers gathered from the whole countryside, tribesmen and townsmen alike, carrying banners and shouting war cries and singing songs of triumph.

I was talking with Fatima soon after the tragedy (from my point of view) had occurred.

She said, "It is very simple, Om John. Life and death don't mean anything to an Arab. Everyone is born, sooner or later everyone dies. What matters is one's honor."

This was the point of view of all the Arabs in the country. The Sheikh had done the inevitable thing. It was as simple as that.

Years before, I had heard the story of a young desert tribesman whose sister had erred and brought disgrace on the family name. The young man avoided the sheikhs' tents in his district, knowing that he would not be offered coffee while there was a stain on the family honor. He pursued the evildoers and eventually killed both his sister and the man who had led her astray. He then rode his horse to the reception tent—the mejliss—of his own sheikh, entered and took his place among the guests and was served coffee as a matter of course. He had wiped out the stain and vindicated the family's good name, and could once more claim his place and be accepted in honorable society.

This concern for the honor of the family is by no means confined to the upper classes of society. It reaches right down to the rock bottom of the social system. I was once involved myself in an "affair of honor," and realized afresh how deeply integrated in the pattern of Arab family life the whole concept of right behavior is.

My husband came in from school one afternoon while I was concluding a long talk on the telephone with one of our British friends, Jim North. He was in charge of the Basrah office of a large American firm which dealt chiefly in dates. My end of the conversation was sufficiently striking to root

John to the spot, and he eavesdropped unashamedly till I hung up.

"Well, upon my word!" he burst out. "Sometimes you amaze even *me*. How in the world do you come to be talking about criminal abortion over the telephone, and to Jim North, of all people—the shyest man in Basrah?"

"Jim has been asking me for my help," I replied with dignity. "He wants my advice about Suffia."

"Suffia! What's the matter with her?"

"That's just what Jim doesn't know. Suffia has disappeared."

Suffia was a gentle, modest young village woman, of mixed Arab and Negro descent, who had worked for me one winter when I wanted extra help in the house. When I no longer needed her, I was happy to recommend her to Betty North, who was looking for someone to help with her two small boys. Betty and the children were now in England for the hot weather, but Suffia was being kept on because she would be needed on their return. She had a room in a row of servants' quarters near the Norths' house, and was flanked on both sides by families of gardeners and boatmen, so presumably she was adequately chaperoned. After she disappeared, Jim began to make inquiries from all the servants and their families.

He was told that she had been having an affair with one of the night watchmen. When he demanded of one of the older and more responsible men why he had not informed his employer of the rumors, he received the classic answer, "I didn't want to trouble you. And anyhow," added the man virtuously. "It might not have been true."

"It's much more trouble to have her disappear," said Jim curtly. "Where do you think she's gone?"

A wealth of theories was eagerly presented to him. The favorite one was that Suffia's family had come in the dead of night, and taken her away and killed her. A second was that she had fled to some remote village down the river where she had friends, to get rid of any consequences there might be of her indiscretion. Another was that she had gone northward somewhere in the desert and claimed sanctuary with Bedouin Arabs.

Others surmised that she had gone down the river on the east side and crossed the Persian border. Her family was connected with the dependents on Sheikh Khazal's domain, and she might well take refuge with some of them.

It was all pure conjecture and Jim North was at his wit's end, how to sift it all out and what course to pursue.

"And what can *you* do about it?" demanded John, after I had given him a summary of the situation.

"I am going to send Zahra."

"Of course!" exclaimed my husband. "What a good idea!"

Zahra was one of my most useful factotums. She and her husband lived in a mat-hut dwelling on the corner of the mission compound where the little settlement for our servants was located. He worked outside, but Zahra did all sorts of jobs for us all. She took care of the little mission church; she cleaned and arranged the rooms where we had our clubs for Arab girls; she prepared the large mat hut which was our mejliss, where we had our meetings for the mothers of our pupils and other neighbors and friends. She set up the tea things for these occasions, got the samovar and brazier to going, and served the little glasses of tea to all comers. She was devoted to our children and was always available as a baby sitter.

But one of her greatest assets to me was as a messenger. She knew where everyone lived and all about them, could ferret out the most inaccessible people and places, and was able to extract information from the most unlikely sources. She was invaluable to me as an "errand girl." (It was many years since she had been a girl, however!) She would deliver my messages correctly, and bring me back definite answers.

Her nose for news made all human contacts interesting to her, but she was especially in her element in any situation which involved doom or disaster.

So, I sent for Zahra, explained the whole situation to her, and as soon as she could arrange her affairs, she set forth on the extremely congenial assignment. She and her husband between them had connections with the dependents of many of the great families of the region and she had acquaintances everywhere. She knew Suffia well and liked her.

She drew her abba around her as I gave her some money for bus and boat fare, and looking like one of the Three Fates, assured me dramatically, "Never fear! I will find Suffia!"

In a few days Zahra was back. She appeared in the doorway of the room where I had one of my sewing classes, and stood still till I looked up. She had a portentous air and was wearing her poker face, which I knew so well. This was not the time, before all these chattering little girls working on their samplers, to discuss the result of her mission. But in response to my lifting my eyebrows in silent question and entreaty, she allowed a flicker to pass over her face which informed me that Suffia was alive and well.

When she had seen the last little Khadijah run down the path, swinging her sewing bag and calling a cheerful farewell, she returned to tell me her tale. With a wealth of detail, and many side excursions into personalities and places, she described her journey from village to village down the river country. Sometimes she went by bus, sometimes in a bellum full of people going home from market, part of the way on foot. I listened patiently, as I was not in suspense about the outcome, and presently we reached the heart of the matter.

Suffia had indeed been summoned to judgment by her family, who had called her to account for getting herself talked about. This is the most disastrous thing that can happen to a young unmarried Moslem woman. Tearfully she assured them that she was innocent of anything except a friendly "Good morning" in reply to the watchman's greeting to her.

"He should never have addressed you," said her father sternly, "and would not have done so if you hadn't encouraged him. Your good name is gone; we shall not be able to arrange a marriage for you with your aunt's son, as we have been planning."

They were somewhat unwillingly convinced of the truth of her protestations, and so instead of taking more drastic measures, they packed Suffia off to a remote village where the date gardens thin out toward the desert, much farther to the south than their own. Here they had relatives, with whom she was to stay indefinitely, in disgrace, and here Zahra eventually found her.

"Do you think she was telling the truth, Zahra?" I asked.

"Oh, Om John, who knows when a person is telling the truth or when she is lying?"

"Who indeed!" I replied bitterly, recalling only too well recent affairs in which we had been involved.

Anyhow, Zahra knew where to find her, and I had something to report to Jim North.

Jim may have been slow of speech, but he was prompt in action. First of all he sent for the night watchman. The man began to explain and to defend his rectitude, and justify himself generally, but Jim cut him short.

"I don't want to know anything about what is past. You have got the girl talked about, and you must put it right. If you will marry her—always supposing she is willing—I will keep you on, and give you married quarters. Otherwise I shall discharge you and send you back upcountry."

The watchman was surprised but acquiescent. There was something vague about a wife up north, but as he was a Moslem it didn't matter. Probably he was pleased at the thought of an agreeable wife on the spot, to cook his food and make him generally comfortable.

Then Jim sent down for Suffia and her father. He put the proposition to them, and asked if she was willing. The father's attitude was "She'd better be!" Suffia gave an answer which is standard in many situations—"As you like." Her submissive attitude, both to her father and to Jim, was quite correct under the circumstances.

"And so the course of true love has run smooth!" I remarked to Jim, with heavy sarcasm, after he had related to me the course of events and the successful conclusion.

He laughed and said in his deliberate way, "Well, I did play the part of fate, I'm afraid, and I hope they live happily ever after!"

I always suspected Jim of having arranged something about a dowry. He and all the other English members of his firm had a paternalistic attitude toward their employees, both in the town office and on their estates, in the best Arab tradition.

Some day I will ask him.

VI

Pleasures and Palaces

The house where Fatima was born was typical of upper-class homes in Basrah fifty years ago. It was on Ashar Creek, the main waterway which led from the river and that section of town called Ashar, to Basrah City—Old Basrah—about two miles away. The second-story bay windows, called *shenasheels,* looked out over the creek; the other side of the house was flush to the street which ran parallel to the creek. This side had few windows, except in the men's section—the diwan. I was always intrigued by the big double doors of these town houses, for most of them had a very small door called the "needle's eye," cut in one of the great doors. This was just large enough for one person to squeeze through, and could be opened without unlocking the main gates. When the large doors were opened, donkeys or even camels could go through them into the courtyard. In the old days, before water was piped into houses, the donkey loaded with waterskins was a daily visitor, bringing sweet water from the river. Camels brought loads of firewood—date branches, and other parts of the tree which were used for fuel—bags of charcoal, and other bulky commodities.

Every door had a brass knocker—the favorite type was a clenched hand. Some houses left the door ajar, and after you had knocked, you could push it open and go in. Many were kept locked, however, especially in my earliest years. The cry would come from inside the house, "Who is it?" and the invariable reply was "I!" I once said to Fatima that I thought this a very uninformative response. She laughed and said, "Oh no, we always recognize the voices of friends or neighbors or tradespeople, and if it is someone strange, we look through the needle's eye before we unlock the gate and let them in."

The wooden bolts could sometimes be raised by a complicated system of strings from within, which could be pulled from the second floor. The house keys were the most enormous I have ever seen—often over a foot in length, and made of iron.

Once you were inside, most houses had an entryway, with another door at right angles, which prevented anyone seeing directly into the women's quarters when the street door was open.

Town houses were as a rule two-storied, and the old-fashioned ones had a fascinating little room called the *kefshkhan,* above the level of the living rooms on the second floor. This was where the Koran reader might sit while the rest of the house was being swept, so that the holy book would not be polluted by dust. Here I have many a time seen Fatima's aunt piously conning the pages of her scriptures, set in front of her on a little folding reading stand.

All roofs were flat, and everyone slept on them in summer. Beds had poles at the corners, and just before sunset, the rolled-up mattresses and bedding would be brought out, beds made up, and the mosquito nets attached firmly to the poles and tucked in tightly around the mattress.

"Be sure to have your servants make the beds before sunset," Fatima's mother advised me when I was a newcomer.

"Otherwise mosquitoes or sand flies will get inside the nets, and your night's rest will be ruined."

I always loved sleeping on the roof. One looked up at the stars through the net; there was a freshness that no air conditioner today can ever approach; and there were night sounds that had a charm all their own. Sometimes I would be wakened by the muffled sound of camel bells, and would sit up in bed and look across the creek from my house and see a long string of camels padding along, dim figures in the starlight. Caravans are not welcome during the daytime on the main road, as they obstruct traffic, and so they usually went through the town by night.

As morning approached there was the dawn prayer call from the nearest mosque; then the Armenian church bell, from the old Christian quarter; and the cooing of innumerable pigeons. Then, as the horizon brightened and the sunrise was imminent, figures appeared on neighboring roofs and mosquito nets were taken down; the sound of plashing from the creek was a sign that boatmen were astir; and the sound of paddles and the swift passage of tiny canoes meant that marsh Arab women were already bringing their buffalo cream and other wares to market.

Most people used a ground-floor room in summer, at least for the afternoon siesta, as it was cooler than the second floor. They usually had a long swinging overhead fan, pulled from outside over a pulley and called a *punkah,* until the days came when electricity made it possible to have mechanical fans.

In winter, people lived in the upstairs rooms, away from the damp. Fatima's family were old-fashioned Arabs, and most of the rooms in their harem, when I first knew them, were furnished in Arab style. There were beautiful rugs on the floor, and all around the walls narrow mattresses and plenty of leaning cushions. The simplicity of this type of room gave a sense of restfulness and leisure.

The Hajji, Fatima's father, had high benches all around

his reception room, with white covers, but I am sure that many of the callers to his diwan sat as men did on the benches in the coffee shops, with their feet tucked under them.

Many of the "first families," the notables—Ashraf in Arabic—were strongly influenced by Turkish taste in their house furnishings. They would have gaudy Brussels carpets, which seemed so regrettable in comparison to the lovely Persian rugs which belonged to the Near East; suites of sofas, armchairs, and straight chairs, always set against the wall in long rows; and elaborately carved tables loaded with bric-a-brac and every sort of ornament. A gramophone with an enormous horn was often to be seen. The head of one of our leading families had a great fancy for music boxes. There was a water bottle which played a tune when lifted from its base; a chair which gave forth music when sat upon; and many other types. Mirrors, large and small, were everywhere, many with elaborate gilded or inlaid frames. One enterprising vizier of a local sheikh took a business-and-pleasure trip to Europe (they did sometimes, even in those far-off days) and was greatly taken with the dressmakers' dummies which he saw in large department stores. He bought several of these *madamas,* as they called them, life-size, and they occupied positions of pride now in the reception rooms of his master and himself.

Country houses were similar to the ones in town, though they tended to be larger and more spread out. My sheikha friend, whom I used to visit down the river, had a one-story house in her country village. The courtyard was enormous, and it was here that the beds were put for summer sleeping, and not on the roof.

As you went down in the social scale, the housing altered. Comfortably off middle-class people would reserve one room at the entrance of the house for the man of the family. These would be merchants, lawyers, doctors, teachers, and government officials not in the highest position. Many of our school-girls came from this group.

Down a little lower in the income scale, a family would sublet part of a house and screen it off to secure privacy, or occupy a tiny house in a more congested part of town where the housing units were small. I learned to know the people of this social level well when I began to do clubwork—one day a week to each group—instead of schoolwork. The girls' school had grown and developed so much that it needed a single woman as principal who had no family responsibilities and could give it her full time and energy. I then took up club-work for less privileged girls who could not be spared from household duties more than one forenoon a week, and I found it absorbing and rewarding. The people in this stratum of society were thriftier than the very poorest of the poor; they were without the aspirations and pretensions of the white-collar class just above them, or the vices and inhumanities of some of the very rich. They asked nothing better than to make an honest living and live at peace with their neighbors, and were really the backbone of the cities of Iraq. They comprised small shopkeepers, policemen, carpenters and other artisans, watchmen and messengers in business concerns, and petty landowners up and down the creeks. The womenfolk were straightforward and down-to-earth, hard-working, and with a zest for life and a humor that made them very companionable. They extracted drama from the smallest happenings of everyday life, and were buoyant and outgoing. These families were ambitious for their sons to be educated, and later for their daughters, but without any illusions of grandeur. It was a joy to teach their little girls to sew and knit and to participate in organized play.

Poor people in the town would often rent one room per family in a house. One such large rambling old-fashioned dwelling, where I used to go to visit one of my girls, had formerly belonged to a prominent family. They had gone down in the world and dispersed all their property, and the formerly fine house was now occupied by fifteen families. Each had one room and made their kitchen arrangements in various corners of the courtyard and verandas. They all shared the roof and the exceedingly antiquated and inadequate sanitary facilities.

On the edge of town, and in the nearby villages, many poor people lived in one-story mud houses, and many others in mat or reed huts called *serifas*. These were usually built in one-, two-, or three-room units grouped around a large central yard, which was enclosed with a mat fence or mud walls. When the family was thrifty and the womenfolk good managers, these serifas could be extremely comfortable and cozy. Fatima's father had an overseer for one of his date plantations who had a delightful establishment in their village down the river. This was the family into which Khadijah had married, the girl whose wedding I had attended in Basrah soon after Fatima's, and I greatly enjoyed going down to visit her and the large sociable group of country cousins. When I pushed open the outer door leading into the farmyard, I would be greeted by the clucking of hens, the quacking of ducks and the honking of geese. The family cow in the corner would often add her *moo-oo*. Bedding was usually airing in the sun, and clothes hung on lines to dry. The old grandmother would be sitting in a sheltered corner spinning wool, from one of their own sheep, on a hand spindle. After the customary prolonged exchange of salutations, we would all go into the main serifa, now furnished with all Khadijah's marriage equipment. Her date-stick bed was in one corner, neatly spread with red cotton quilts, and the gay tin trunks around the sides of the room. We seated ourselves on white-covered cushions on the floor, while Khadijah and her mother-in-law bustled around getting the tea glasses arranged and the brazier glowing. The mud floor was covered with woolen rugs—*basaats,* or *ghalims,* they were called. The serifa was well built, with several thicknesses of mats for both walls and roof, and was weatherproof and waterproof. Nothing could be more comfortable and snug on a crisp winter afternoon.

Not all serifas were well built, however, nor were all their occupants thrifty. On the edge of town there were many areas which were dreary slums. The very poor could not afford enough mats to make their huts weatherproof or to keep them in repair, and in many cases they were not even an adequate shelter. There was little privacy and no sanitation. The water supply was the creeks, where women washed their dishes and their vegetables, their clothes and their children, and which were used as lavatories.

Serifa villages were a fire hazard, and the hapless occupants were frequently burned out. During one winter (more than twenty years ago) I twice supplied some of my poorest club girls with quilts and blankets, when their families lost everything in successive fires.

When these serifa settlements were on low ground, there was also danger of floods in the springtime. Before extensive irrigation and flood-control engineering projects were carried out in the north of Iraq, melting snows in the mountains of Kurdistan and Turkey caused the Tigris and Euphrates rivers to overflow every spring. One year the entire city of Baghdad was threatened with complete destruction by flood. The marshes between the rivers in lower Iraq became a sea, and whole villages were inundated and had to be evacuated.

We Basrah residents suffered severe damage to our houses and the loss of all our gardens. Except for the lordly date palms, all vegetation was destroyed in this disastrous year. Grape arbors, rose gardens, fruit trees, oleanders and Persian lilac trees, and all the vegetable gardens were killed. Of course the unfortunate serifa dwellers suffered most, and large-scale relief had to be undertaken. Health hazards followed in the wake of the floods, especially when the waters receded and left a thick scum of decaying vegetation.

Flood-control projects on a large scale have now removed this annual danger. The fire risks of serifas led to legislation requiring that they all be plastered with mud on the outside walls; and in some areas mat dwellings were prohibited. Mud huts replaced them in many places, and as time went on, neat rows of brick housing developments were built all over the countryside for the working classes.

Out on the desert the nomads or seminomads among the Bedouin lived in tents which could be moved as they shifted to follow pasturage for their camels or sheep. The desert encampments followed a distinct pattern, sometimes in a circle but more often in rows. The Sheikh's tent faced the direction from which possible guests or enemies might approach, and was easily recognizable, as it was the largest one. The group of women's tents would be far away enough for privacy, but near enough for protection. The ruling sheikhs often had town houses in the nearest city, and lived there for part of the year at least, sometimes in great magnificence.

Two thirds of the population of Iraq live in rural areas, and so it is sometimes called a land of villages. The villagers, who were usually originally of nomad origin, had gradually given up the breeding of camels and later on of sheep and goats, for farming. Villages ranged in population from two hundred to two thousand or more, and were (and still are) almost entirely agricultural. The houses are tightly packed together, and are constructed chiefly of mud reinforced with straw or cow dung. Furniture is of the simplest—mats, storage chests, and sometimes date-stick bedsteads. Lighting at night is provided by oil lamps and lanterns or by a fire. This was the pattern of living in the agricultural communities fifty years ago, and in many isolated areas it has hardly changed up to the present time. Traditional modes of behavior and thought still prevail.

The rural town, as distinguished from the large village, has a more varied population and a wider social and economic range. Here are to be found moderately well-to-do people, and a few comparatively wealthy landowners or merchants, whose houses are much more spacious and better constructed than those of the majority, who live in poverty.

The marsh Arabs, or Madaan—the People of the Reeds—lived in huts made of reeds, raised water buffaloes, and went about in canoes. I was always reminded of American Indian squaws when I saw these erect, unveiled marsh Arab women expertly paddling their little canoes on their way to and from the marshlands where they lived.

Transportation in the old days, when I first knew Basrah, was largely by water. There was one road between Ashar, the part of town along the river, and Basrah City—sometimes called Old Basrah—a mile or two inland. (Fatima lived in Ashar near the beginning of the creek, and I lived farther along the creek toward Basrah City.) Villages were strung along this road like beads on a chain. The road was a sea of mud during the winter rains, and thick with dust all the rest of the year. Open carriages drawn by dispirited-looking horses used this road; brisk donkeys with their bells jingling; and disdainful camels with their heads high. We took carriages if the tide was too low to go to Basrah City by bellum, but otherwise everyone used those most comfortable boats. They combined the best features of a gondola and a canoe, and took us everywhere, on the creeks and up and down the river. In summer they were equipped with jaunty awnings to protect their passengers from the sun. For a long trip, such as the distance between Basrah and Abul Khassib, launches were in common use.

Many places could be reached only on foot, on raised paths through the date gardens, with perilous date-log bridges which had to be negotiated, and we all walked much more in those days than in later years. After roads were built and motorcars became increasingly available, country places became much more accessible.

Buses came into use after the main roads were paved, some-where in the nineteen thirties, and I soon began to use them for the short trip between Ashar and Basrah City. John de-plored my fondness for riding in buses, and would say ur-gently when I set out from home, "Please, take a taxi today!" I used to threaten that I would sometime go third class by train to Baghdad, in a women's compartment. There, I would indeed have "seen life," for whole families traveled with their bedding and their pots and pans and samovars, and the socia-bility of those crowded, noisy railway carriages was most in-triguing. I would have loved a trip by day. Unfortunately it was an overnight journey to Baghdad, and even my hardy spirit quailed at the thought of sitting up all night on a hard wooden bench, amid crying babies, loud talking, women smoking, and dozens of small children with regrettably primi-tive hygienic habits.

But the bus, for short trips, was an entirely different matter. "I'll take a taxi if the buses are crowded," I would assure my husband. I always went to the terminal and would take my place in an empty bus, and have the fun of watching it fill up, chiefly with village Arabs and countryfolk, and hear the inter-change of salty remarks and see all the byplay. One day a woman with a huge market basket of groceries and green vegetables had topped it off with a gigantic fish, tail protrud-ing.

"You can't bring that in here!" shouted the driver. "It takes up too much room, and the fish smells terrible!"

"Oh yes, I can!" shrilled the woman, scrambling aboard. "All the world carry fish with them in buses and carriages!"

There was a brisk argument and she stowed her basket near the entrance, where everyone stumbled over it. While the driver was still grumbling, a man came along with an enor-mous basket containing live chickens with their feet tied to-gether. They were squawking and flapping their wings and he had difficulty in hoisting the basket up when his turn came in the line of shoving passengers.

"This cannot be!" roared the driver. "It must be!" was the emphatic answer as the chickens were pushed aboard. Then a really epic altercation took place, in which the passengers joined, offering advice and trying to soothe the antagonists when they began cursing each other's parents. Eventually the owner of the chickens paid an extra fare, under protest, the basket was pushed into the aisle, and several small children began to howl with fright at the unholy noise the chickens made.

Then with a grinding of gears we were off, and trundled along the road beside the creek, dropping passengers and picking up others, all the way to Basrah City.

My return that day afforded drama to those in the bus with me, instead of my being a mere observer as I usually was. I went to our girls' school to get the large life-sized rubber baby doll that I used for demonstration in my Child Welfare classes. He was named Yahya—the Arab form for John, and he had been bathed and dressed many times before groups of admiring club girls. I had loaned him to the girls' school, but needed him unexpectedly, and had gone to fetch him. I decided that the easiest way to carry him was as though he were a real baby: it seemed impossible to make a parcel of him. He was dressed in Arab baby clothes, cap and all, made by the club girls. I walked through the back streets to the nearest bus stop, and heard murmurs and speculation from people I passed. Once on the bus, I settled him on my lap, where even to me he felt like a real baby. I could sense the ripple of interest and surmise that went through the bus, and heard low questions behind me— "Is that a living child, or could it be a doll?"

I finally relieved the curiosity of my fellow passengers, and said to the general public, "This is not a real baby, but I use him to show my pupils how to take care of a real baby."

The captive audience at once requested a demonstration, and I held them spellbound while I delivered an impromptu lecture in the best Dr. Spock manner.

"Why don't you have him swaddled?" demanded an old woman, whose grandchild was standing between her knees, gazing fascinated at the face of the smiling doll.

"We believe in leaving their limbs free," I replied, and upon demand revealed Yahya's diapers. If my bus stop had not been imminent, I should have been obliged to show them several times how the diapers were pinned, instead of giving only one hasty performance. When I alighted, they all shouted cheerful good-bys and blessings, and the old crone who had asked about swaddling bands yelled after me, "I shall send my granddaughter to you when she is old enough!"

Arab womenfolk are sociable and gregarious, and many and varied were the parties in that far-off time before the days of cars.

One of my earliest excursions was an all-day trip to Zobeir, given in honor of the wife of the new Turkish governor. The wives of one of our leading citizens were the hostesses, and all the elite of Basrah were invited. Zobeir is a desert town nearly ten miles west of the river, and we went perforce in carriages over the desert track. An element of excitement was added by our escort of several mounted Turkish policemen, a necessary precaution in those days. They rode their horses round and round our cavalcade, occasionally firing off their rifles from sheer exuberance. This terrified some of the less-traveled ladies of the party, who would exclaim "Robbers!" and peer around fearfully as they pulled their veils over their faces.

The trip itself was enjoyable and novel. Many of us had never been to Zobeir before, and we were intrigued with the desert as Basrah and its date palms receded, and Sinbad's Tower grew taller and nearer. This is the first landmark of Zobeir, undoubtedly only legendary but of romantic interest.

The town shone before us on the desert, a lofty minaret marking the great mosque. All the houses here were one-storied, like my friend the Sheikha's, down the river. We climbed down from our carriages and streamed into a huge courtyard where we were welcomed by our hostesses—our Basrah friends, and their relatives of Zobeir.

Several of the guests, as well as some of the ladies giving the party, were of Turkish extraction, and normally wore European clothes with their own modifications. But on this occasion, they had all been told to wear Arab dress, complete with traditional jewelry, and it was a great sight when the whole company shed their black veils and abbas and appeared in all their glory. Every color of the rainbow appeared in their charming flowing robes; and the glitter of gold which flashed from their splendid ornaments made the precaution of the mounted guard who had escorted us over the desert seem a very wise arrangement. The assemblage would have been well worth the attention of a daring robber band of desert tribesmen.

The only person present in European dress besides myself was the guest of honor!

Fatima's mother edged her way through the crowd to speak to me. We hadn't been in the same carriage driving out, but she knew that I had been to pay an official call on the governor's lady, a few days before this party.

"Which one is the Khanum from Turkey?" she hissed in my ear. "I don't see her anywhere."

"Over there, talking to Om Bedr," I said, indicating a little group of our hostesses and the ladies of the house where we were.

"*That* one?" exclaimed Om Fatima in deep disappointment. "Why, she is no more dressed up than you are—just like a Derwish!"

A Derwish is a mendicant, and I was secretly amused and not in the least offended, as I had often been told frankly by my intimates that it was a pity I dressed so simply, and wore no conspicuous jewelry. The lady from Constantinople, as it was then called, wore a pretty afternoon dress, plain in cut and dark in color, which might well have come from Paris, via a French shop in the Turkish capital, but which was insignificant to Arab eyes among all these birds of paradise. Her only jewelry was her wedding ring and a wrist watch.

"She's a *very* nice person," I said encouragingly.

"Can she talk any Arabic?" demanded Om Fatima suspiciously.

"Enough to get on with. She has been with her husband in Arab posts before."

Tall glasses of sherbet were now passed around, in pierced silver holders, and then everyone settled down for a chat while we waited for our dinner. This was a Gargantuan Arab feast, served in a second courtyard. I had never before seen so many whole roasted sheep as were placed on the long white cloth, each on its own tray. The repast was spread on the floor, as was customary in those days, but my fellow "Derwish" and I were given cushions to sit on, and as a further concession were provided with forks and spoons. I was grateful for this, because I hadn't yet learned to be as expert at eating with my fingers as I later became, and apparently neither had the governor's wife!

After the meal, Negro serving women poured water over our hands from graceful ewers into a bowl—both of exquisitely chased Persian silver—and wiped our hands on gold-embroidered towels. I had seen similar ones in Fatima's bridal outfit and wondered when people ever used anything so elaborate. Now I knew! Rose water was then sprinkled over the guests' hands and handkerchiefs, from matching silver containers. Everyone relaxed while tea was served, and the little glasses of strong sweet tea were most refreshing after the heavy meal.

Then, before our return to Basrah, many of the ladies

wanted to visit the shrine of Zobeir, for whom the town was named, and the Sunni cemetery adjacent where all Basrah notables of that sect were buried. Zobeir was a cousin of the Prophet Mohammed, and was one of the ten to whom Mohammed gave certain assurances of Paradise.

Messages then came in from the gendarmes who had escorted us, who had been generously fed in the men's quarters in the meantime, urging us to make ready for the return trip.

"The Pasha [who was the Commandant of Police] said we must be sure to have all the noble ladies back within the gates of Basrah before sunset," was the word that was relayed to us.

No one had any wish to encounter robbers on the desert after dark, so with all speed the outer garments were produced, sorted out, put on and adjusted, and we were on our way.

Another social event of that first year which stands out vividly in my memory was my first and only visit to a Turkish bath. I was invited by the mother of a great friend of John's who had taken me under her wing when I first arrived in Basrah. She herself was a Circassian, with a Turkish background, and had been in the Imperial harem in Constantinople as a child and a young girl. She was given as a present to a Basrah Pasha, then in the Turkish capital, who in turn gave her to an Arab friend in Basrah whom he wished to honor. She was legally married to him and her son became a prominent personage in the region. I used to be fascinated by her tales of life in the Sultan's harem, where she and several hundred other girls were trained and educated. They learned to play the 'Ud—the lute—and many other arts of pleasing.

Her daughter-in-law was a recent bride and I was included in one of the parties, then so popular, to a Turkish bath. I accepted joyfully and ignorantly, since I knew what a social center the *hammams,* as the baths were called, were; but I was not realistic enough, in my youth and inexperience, to picture exactly what was involved. We set out from my friends' house followed by servants loaded with impedimenta —towels galore, silver bowls to pour the water over us, boxes for our jewelry, *bukshas* for our clothes, lounging robes, a whole equipment for making tea, and last of all the grinning little black girl with her mistress' water pipe—the ubiquitous hubble-bubble.

When we went in, we were divested of our outer garments in an anteroom. After that, we entered the first of the long succession of rooms of the hammam, and were rapidly divested of all the rest of our clothes. I had realized of course that one can't take a bath with clothes on, but I had vaguely pictured a little cubicle where the attendant perhaps came in and rubbed your back, and where you dressed again. Never had I visualized a large room, with troughs and faucets around the sides, filled with women and children strolling around unconcernedly without one stitch of clothes on. We were joyfully hailed by our friends and welcomed to the bath, when we entered the large room in the same state of nature as all the rest of them. Once I had accepted the situation, and made the rapid psychological adjustment which was necessary, I settled down and enjoyed myself. The room was filled with clouds of steam and smoke from many cigarettes; noisy with children crying loudly because they had soap in their eyes, friends calling to each other above the din, and the bath attendants shouting orders and directions. We progressed to hot, hotter, and hottest, in the successive rooms; were scrubbed by the bath attendants with castile soap and a sort of harsh sponge called a *loofah,* till the flesh nearly came off our bones; had our hair vigorously shampooed, first with a kind of mud—*tene khawa*—local to the region and supposed to be very good for the hair and scalp, and then again with soap, and finally much rinsing. We went back in reverse order, were pummeled and massaged, lying on slabs, and at long last we were dried with warm towels. Finally we were wrapped in huge robes, and sank down on cushions in a room where one of the hostess' servants had cinnamon tea ready for us. Oh, how good it tasted, and how relaxed and refreshed we were! Friends joined us, we heard the latest news and the raciest gossip, and had a most leisurely social time.

When I got home John asked me cheerily, "Well, did you have a good time?"

I turned on him and demanded, "Why didn't you let me know what I was in for, and warn me?"

He replied with perfect justice, "How would I know what Arab ladies do?"

However, I admitted to him that I had really enjoyed the experience very much, and that I had certainly seen a lot of my friends.

Another joy of both my earlier and later years was Ramadhan visiting. Ramadhan is the fasting month of the Moslem calendar, when all the faithful are supposed to refrain from food and drink during the day. This begins in the morning when there is light enough for a black thread to be discernible from a white one, and ends with the gun which is fired off at sunset. A person who is fasting may not smoke, take medicine, have drops put in his eyes, or even swallow his own saliva.

The Moslem calendar follows the lunar months, so that every year the month is about eleven days earlier than in the preceding year. This results in a complete cycle every thirty-three years, and so Ramadhan was sometimes in winter and sometimes in summer. The long hot days of summer made fasting a burden, but the compensation was the pleasure of sitting on the roof, or in an open courtyard, for the evening visitations.

Most of my women friends fasted, and the whole of life was geared to a changed routine during this month. They got as much sleep as they could during the day, between the performance of their household duties, and real living began with the sunset gun. My friends would take a drink—fruit juice in summer, tea in winter, or perhaps only water. Then they said their prayers, and after that nearly everyone would light a cigarette and sit down with a great sigh of relief. The Fitur—the Breaking of the Fast—which is the evening meal, would follow at their leisure. Certain delicacies were peculiar to this season, and the bazaars were always more plentifully stocked then than at any other season of the year. A kind of spun sugar candy called Maidens' Hair was made only during Ramadhan.

After the Breaking of the Fast, a long tea drinking would follow, and this was the time when friends would drop in and plans would be made for the remainder of the night. Religious readings were always held regularly on Ramadhan nights, and everyone attended at least once a week. The Koran should be read through by every believer during this month, and some of the large houses had their own Mullahs, who would sit at night in the entrance to the men's quarters intoning the holy book in a clear loud voice that could be heard throughout the whole establishment. Fatima and I used to visit one family where there was a large and merry group of sisters, with a delightful vivacious mother who became one of my special friends. Above the cheerful babble of voices in their great reception room, the rattle of tea glasses and coffee cups, the greetings of guests arriving and the salutations of those taking their leave, it was impressive to hear in the distance the clear bell-like tones of the Mullah chanting the Koran.

I used to go out about three evenings a week during Ramadhan, and sometimes oftener. My family took a very unsympathetic view of my activities. They said that my digestion was upset by the irregular meals I ate at unusual

The author and her son John in Arab dress, 1917

My old Zahra

A residential street of long ago

Maqam Mosque on Ashar Creek with bellums in the foreground

Coolie women of the Khawat Rezna tribe carrying brick

Doorway to our girls' school, with hand-wrought brass knockers and needle's-eye door

A class in the Baghdad Teachers' Training College, 1953

Net-ball at the School of Domestic Science, 1954

Two little school girls in the early days

Basrah, "the Venice of the East"

Picnic parties on a pleasant waterway

times, and that my disposition was unfavorably affected by the hours I kept.

I never knew whether I would eat only fruit and sweets during the course of the night, along with many glasses of tea and cups of coffee, or whether I would encounter a large and lavish meal somewhere at midnight or later. So I formed the habit of taking a cup of soup while my children were having their early supper, just to be on the safe side.

John would come into the dining room and say in a martyred tone, "Where are you going tonight?"

"Out with Fatima," I would reply gaily.

"To whose house?"

"I don't know, she was waiting to hear if her cousins would be up from Abul Khassib. If they do come we will probably go to the Khalf girls. And the Hajjia says we ought to go to Sayyid Khadheir's, because there has been a death in the family, and everyone is going there to condole with them."

"What time do you think you will get home?"—hopefully.

"I have no idea!"—unhelpfully.

Wherever we went, we would encounter on the street groups of black-cloaked and veiled women, escorted by a servant carrying a lantern, going or coming from visits or readings. The streets at two in the morning were as lively as at two in the afternoon during the rest of the year.

A great social institution which developed after Iraq became independent, in the early nineteen thirties, was At Homes, Kabools in Arabic. Perhaps society became a little more organized and complicated then; anyhow, most of the leading families had their appointed days, every week or twice a month, and that was when we knew we would find our friends at home. By this time, almost every house had at least one room furnished with heavy overstuffed furniture, whatnots, and tables loaded with *objets d'art*. But there was always an adjoining room in the old style, for guests who preferred to sit on the floor. Here the visitors would leave their toe slippers outside the door and tuck their stockinged feet under them, leaving the large sofas and chairs in the next room for fine ladies who wore high-heeled slippers and silk stockings, and everything else to correspond.

In spring and summer, we knew the delights of out-of-door parties in the date gardens. The fresh green of willows and Persian lilacs, and the gorgeous blossoming oleanders on the banks of the river and the canals, made all our waterways vistas of loveliness in April and May. The bellums were the pleasantest possible means of transportation, and at this time of year the tide was always high. The winter snows had melted in the faraway mountains in the north, the Tigris and Euphrates rivers were brimming full, and our own Arab River, the Shatt-el-Arab, was near to flood level.

Many families had little summer houses in their country date orchards, and would send the samavor and other tea things off by a servant, ahead of time, and then fill a bellum with friends and pole down the river and up Khorah Creek or one of the other canals which crisscrossed the whole region outside the town. Here we would drink our tea in a grape arbor, under tall majestic date palms. Orange blossoms were coming out then, and their sweetness was almost overpowering. Pomegranate trees were just coming into bloom, and the brilliant crimson flowers made a startling splash of color against the green foliage.

Sometimes it would be an all-day party, if we went to gardens at some distance, and a gardener's wife would cook us a succulent fish dinner in one of her out-of-door ovens.

The desert was beautiful in spring, too, for all sorts of wild flowers came into bloom after the winter rains. The loveliest were tiny iris, which made a perfect carpet of deep blue for great stretches. Clumps or groves of tamarisk trees, something like pines, were like little oases and made ideal picnic spots. After motorcars came into general use, desert picnics were the favorite form of spring outing for rich and poor alike. Interrelated families would charter a bus and pack everyone in, from the old grandmother to the newest baby, for a day in the great open spaces.

On several occasions my co-worker and I had the hardihood to take parties of our club girls on these excursions to the desert. They were wild with delight, for it was a rare treat to these children who lived in city streets. They would promise, before we set out, to be as quiet as mice in the bus, and as good as gold all day. But on the way from Basrah to Zobeir, their overflowing spirits would get the better of them. Someone always had a little drum and would thrum on it as Negro women did at weddings; the whole group would clap their hands rhythmically; and they would sing at the top of their lungs. As we approached Zobeir, through which we had to pass to get to the desert beyond, I would beg them to quiet down, and remind them of their solemn promises. The appeal to them as Arab girls, who should be demure and inconspicuous, fell on deaf ears. They were good-natured but incorrigible, and I could only hope that we would get through the town without anyone recognizing us. Once out on the desert, they had all the scope they wanted, and romped and played, ate and drank and napped and played again, to their hearts' content for a whole long day.

The cinema came to Basrah early in the nineteen twenties and was immediately popular, as it has been ever since. The first one opened in a rickety old building with a poor projector and a very inferior type of film, but was enthusiastically patronized. More and better-appointed ones soon followed, and ladies' days were instituted at once. Among the more progressive families, cinema parties became a popular form of entertainment. The old-fashioned held out against it, and I happened to be present at a most amusing social crisis in the family of some very good friends of mine. The mother was a strong-minded and determined woman who had brought up her family of daughters strictly and well.

The younger girls had been my pupils in years past. There was one son, an exemplary young man who had just married a delightful girl. While Om Suliman and I were sitting talking one day at her house, her daughter-in-law came into the room, followed rather timidly by two of the girls.

"Om Suliman," said the young wife deferentially, after she had greeted me, "an invitation has just come for us to go to the cinema this afternoon with the family of Hajji Ibrahim. Om Ahmed—his wife—is going, and all the girls, and also the family of Seyyid Tahir, their relatives."

"Certainly not!" was the vigorous reply. "Your father would never allow it. Others may take up with these loose modern ways, but we do not."

"But, my mother," put in one of the girls eagerly, "Baba [the family name for Papa] has already given his permission, if you are willing."

Om Suliman was furious, but recognized defeat when she saw it. Her husband was a gentle and kindly soul who had always felt that she was inclined to be too strict with the girls, and evidently their shrewd move of applying to him first, emboldened him to take a stand in their behalf.

"All right, go!" she shouted. "Let it be said that the family of Tewfiq Effendi have left off their modesty! Next, we shall hear that they are considered streetwalkers." (She used a much more offensive term.)

The girls scuttled out, but the daughter-in-law stayed behind.

"Om Suliman," she said earnestly and sweetly, "if you feel so strongly about it, I don't want to go. I will talk to the girls, and we will refuse the invitation."

"No, no," said the older woman crossly, "it is the father of the family who makes the decisions."

So Saliha joined her young sisters-in-law in the next room, and I could see them getting out their abbas and veils. They were all of them relieved, I heard afterward, that I happened to be on the spot to bear the brunt of Om Suliman's first wrath and indignation. They knew that I was detached but sympathetic; and I got a special message from Tewfiq Effendi, thanking me for soothing and somewhat mollifying his irate wife before he had to encounter her himself.

During one of the earliest years of the cinema, a Bible film, based on stories from the Old Testament, was advertised. My colleague, who was now principal of our girls' school, had been besieged by some of her older pupils to chaperon them to the pictures, as their families would allow them to go with her but with no one else. She thought the story of Joseph sounded suitable, and accordingly shepherded quite a group to the next Ladies' Day. She was dismayed to discover, as the play began, that the episode of Joseph in Potiphar's house in Egypt was the theme. Potiphar's wife was depicted as a luscious temptress, and as the play developed, it became increasingly graphic and less and less suitable for sheltered young girls to see. At last it reached a point where the outraged chaperon passed the word down the line that the girls were to put on their abbas and follow her out. They were rebellious at heart, for they were enjoying themselves beyond their wildest anticipations, but they were disciplined and obedient, and accordingly trailed out disconsolately behind their teacher's erect and indignant figure. Next day, all the harems of Basrah rang with praise and approval for the way in which the headmistress of the American school guarded her charges from demoralizing influences.

More and better cinemas were opened as time went on, and good and bad pictures were available to all. Egyptian films were the favorites, with familiar backgrounds, and with subtitles (and later, dialogue) in Arabic, but all kinds were enthusiastically attended.

A friend of ours once came down from Amarah, a trip of a little over a hundred miles, in record time, because the driver of his taxi wanted to be in Basrah in time to see *Tarzan!*

[101]

VII

May Your Table Always Be Spread

"May your table always be spread" is the phrase, much more graceful in Arabic than in the English translation, which is always murmured by the guest to an Arab host on rising after a meal.

Arab hospitality is proverbial, and their tables are indeed always spread for their friends. From the humblest tent on the desert to the sheikh's lordly pavilion, from the smallest serifa in a date garden to the many-roomed palace of the wealthy landowner, you can be sure of a glass of tea or a cup of coffee, freshly baked bread with a handful of dates, or a sumptuous meal. No visitor, even the most transient caller, is allowed to leave the house without partaking of hospitality. I learned early, the hard way, not to go inside the women's quarters and sit down, unless I was prepared to stay while tea was got ready, or a glass of sherbet (the Arabic word for any fruit drink) or some other form of refreshment. If I had an errand that could be dispatched briefly, I stood inside the street door and delivered my message, and then, amid protests, went on my way. If I entered the domestic circle I must have leisure enough to observe the usages of social intercourse, otherwise I was violating their sense of the courtesy due to a guest, and showing myself insensitive to old and honorable traditions.

The feast at Zobeir was the first party of that magnitude which I had ever attended, and I can still recall my amazement at the quantity and variety of the food, laid out in such profusion that you could hardly see the long white cloths on which the banquet was spread. Each whole roasted sheep was embedded in rice, some of it flavored and tinted with saffron, and some with which the sheep was stuffed containing almonds and raisins and a subtle blend of spices and herbs. Chickens, either roasted or in stews, were much in evidence; innumerable dishes of various kinds of stew flanked the larger platters. This was my first experience with truffles, a delicacy something like mushrooms, which grow under the surface of the desert only in a year when there are early rains to crack the dry top soil. They are delicious in stews, sliced and fried by themselves, or cold as a salad. Several years later, during one season when they were especially plentiful, I had served them at my own table in as many ways as I could think of, and I looked in my faithful Fannie Farmer cookbook for new suggestions. All that she had to tell me was: "Truffles are imported from the south of France, and are far too expensive for ordinary use"!

Croquettes figured in the Zobeir feast, some of rice, others called *kubba burghil,* made of the famous cracked wheat of the north, mixed with ground mutton, onion, raisins, and almonds. The great stand-by *dolma* was there in profusion—grape leaves wrapped around rice and mutton, delicately seasoned, and cooked by steaming. There was stuffed eggplant, stuffed cucumber, stuffed marrow, and stuffed cabbage. Cauliflower appeared in stews, or fried crisply. Great bowls of Arab pickles, homemade, pungent with spices and surely among the most delectable in the world, yoghurt with sliced cucumbers and garlic, and fresh salad of raw tomatoes, green onions, chopped mint and parsley, added zest to all these rich and heavy foods. Big pitchers of buttermilk went well with the meal, and at every place was a great round of fresh, crisp Arab bread.

For dessert there were oranges, bananas and dates, and a soup plate apiece (if one had room for it) of a milk pudding called *muhalliby,* made with rice flour and delicately flavored with cardamom and rose water. There were other sweets, too, made with date syrup, and an assortment of tempting pastries.

I remarked on the abundance to Om Fatima as we were drinking our tea afterward, and she said, "You should have seen tribal feasts in the old days! This is nothing! The Hajji has told me of a whole roasted camel—a young and tender one. It was stuffed with sheep, the sheep with turkeys, the turkeys with quail, and the quail with larks!"

I groaned at her description, for at the moment I didn't feel as though I could ever face even a whole roast sheep again.

"This was a good meal," she continued reflectively. "It is hard to cook well for so many people. The kubba burghil was a little greasy, it should be quite dry. Mine is better, you must let me make it for you some day. Have you ever had a meal with Om Hussein, my partner wife? She lived in the north as a girl and she knows Turkish dishes. She is a good cook," she added generously.

Later on I did become well acquainted with Om Hussein, the childless wife of Hajji Izzat, and had many a pleasant meal with her. She introduced me to *burag,* little savory fried pastries, and *sanbusik,* famous in Syria—baked turnovers with a sweet or a savory filling. She made many kinds of pilau, different versions of rice.

A family with a Persian background loved to prepare one

of their specialties for me, *fasinjan*. This was duck or chicken, served with a thick rich sauce made of pounded walnut meats and pomegranate juice, delicious beyond description. They also did an excellent chicken pilau, the rice garnished with fried onions, almonds, and currants.

But the best pilau I ever ate was at a picnic meal on the desert between Kuwait and Basrah. I had been paying a visit to Kuwait and was returning to Basrah by car. This was in the early 1930's, long before the days of oil, and Kuwait was just a little walled Arab city at the head of the Persian Gulf, between the desert and the sea. We found it novel and exciting to be able to get to and fro from Basrah by car, because in my very early days Kuwait was accessible only by the British India ships, which stopped there once in two weeks, and the journey from Basrah was at least overnight. Now, to reach it in three or four hours by car, traveling on a reasonably good desert road of not much over a hundred miles, seemed like the magic carpet.

(In 1947 my husband and I did it by airplane in twenty minutes. As he peered out of the plane windows after we left Kuwait, John exclaimed to me, "To think that when I did this on horseback in 1909, we thought we made wonderfully good time because we did it in three days!")

On this trip by car, made memorable by the pilau, I had engaged one place in a taxi, as we always did, not knowing who my fellow passengers might be. I received word the night before that it would be filled by Arab ladies whom I knew well, returning to Basrah after a visit to relatives in Kuwait. I expressed a hope that we could leave by nine o'clock, and the reply came back "In sha'Allah"—"If God wills." God did not will (I had feared that He would not) and we did not get away till after eleven. The car was filled to capacity, and at the last moment a Negro serving woman came rushing out of the house and jumped into the back seat of the car, crouching down on the floor. I protested, both on behalf of her comfort and our feet on which she was sitting, but one of the Arab ladies said coolly, "We shall need her to make our tea when we stop for lunch."

Stop for lunch we did, and after they had all prayed their noonday prayers, out in the middle of the desert, they produced a large kettle of the most delicious mutton pilau I had ever tasted. The rice was perfect, the seasoning exactly right, and the pieces of mutton so tender that they fairly melted in our mouths. The covered kettle had been wrapped in many thicknesses of newspaper, so that the contents were still hot. There was fresh Arab bread—one of our last stops in town had been at a bakery—the crisp rounds tied up in a white cloth; and we each had an orange. In the meantime the servant had produced, from a large can tied on the car somewhere, a primus stove and a kettle and all the makings for tea, and this was ready when we had finished our lunch. I was quite reconciled by then to a much later arrival in Basrah than I had hoped for, and I have never forgotten the pleasant and unexpected Arab picnic out in the blue.

Kebab was another stand-by for picnics. *Shish kebab* is now a household word in America, but the Basrah version is a little different. Ours is minced mutton, well seasoned, wrapped around the skewer which is the *shish,* and then grilled over a hot charcoal fire. When done to a turn, it is pulled gently off the skewer and wrapped in a piece of Arab bread, with green onions and parsley or mint.

Fish picnics were extremely popular in both Basrah and Baghdad. Baghdad is famous for *samak masguf,* large fish propped up on wooden sticks, to be grilled on open brushwood fires, somewhere along the river front.

But Basrah folk scorn the river fish, and take delight in the plentiful *siboor* in spring. This is exactly like shad, bones and all, and is in such abundance that both rich and poor can enjoy it. It is split open and spread with a paste of sharp and savory flavors, including curry. It is then grilled on the inside of the conical hollow bread ovens, somewhere out of doors; for weeks in the spring, the tantalizing odor used to greet us whenever we walked abroad. The tiny bones make eating a slow process, and whenever a child is late to school in the afternoon, the teacher's stock question is, "Why are you not on time? Did you have fish for lunch?" Many other kinds of fish are available in Basrah throughout the year, some of it salt-water fish from the Persian Gulf.

Sweets are rich and indigestible and succulent. *Buklawa* is thin layers of pastry, containing pistachio nuts or almonds and dripping with honey. *Burma* is twisted pastry rolls, very short, sometimes containing coconut. *Sirrat el Khatoon,* which means "the lady's navel," is a round of pastry covered with honey, and with a dollop of thick buffalo cream in a central depression.

Salabia look like pretzels, but have a thin crisp coating filled with sweet syrup. *Kalaicha* are similar to little turn-overs, and have a stuffing of dates or chopped nuts.

My Hajjia used to get a woman in before Ramadhan whose specialty was pastry and have her make dozens of these delicacies, to have on hand during the festive evenings of the fasting month.

There was another dish special to this month called *harisa.* Whole wheat and mutton are boiled together till they are almost like a paste, then put through a sieve, and then served with the top covered with melted butter, sugar, and cinnamon.

A pleasant little folk story is told about harisa. A countryman went in to town on business during Ramadhan, and had his evening meal in a restaurant, where this was one of the dishes served to him. He was ecstatic over such a delicacy, which he had never eaten before, and vowed that he would get his wife to learn to make it.

"Now what did you say its name is?" he demanded of the host of the teashop, and repeated "Harisa, harisa, harisa" as he left, and as he traveled toward home the next morning. A few miles from town he had to cross a branch of the river, and paused to water his horse. In his preoccupation with this, he stopped repeating his new word, and found when he set off again that he had forgotten it. He turned his horse back and made him step in the water, exclaiming, "You have made me lose my word in the river, now find it for me!"

Along came a party of horsemen who wanted to water their animals, too, and when they saw how he had stirred up the mud by looking for what he had lost there, they cursed him and said, "What do you mean, riding your horse back and forth until you have made the water like harisa?"

"The mercy of God be upon your parents!" he exclaimed. "You have found my word for me!"

The kitchens of my Arab friends, when I first lived in Basrah, were a source of amazement to me. At that time most cooking was done on charcoal, on open hearths built up on brickwork that was breast-high, or over fires of date branches in an open hole in the courtyard. Nests of saucepans had no handles, but were expertly dealt with nevertheless. Tinned copper was in common use, and huge pots and trays of this metal were in every household. All grains, spices, and meat were crushed or ground at home, so several mortars and pestles of varying sizes were essential. A mill made of two grindstones, one above the other, was used for wheat, because many people ground their own flour for bread. The low grinding sound could be heard, from behind the matting walls, when one passed through the byways of a serifa village, and in the kitchen courtyards of large houses. How thrilling it was to be told that this was the selfsame mill mentioned so often in the Bible, as far back as the Book of Exodus.

A round wooden table only a few inches high, complete with a low stool and a long thin rolling pin, was not only a baking board, but was also used for chopping meat.

Water was brought daily in goatskins, either on a donkey's back or that of a waterman—the indispensable *saqqa*. It was kept in large unglazed pottery jars with a wide top and pointed base supported on a wooden framework. The water was chilled by evaporation from the porous sides, and would ooze through and drip into a vessel placed below. Small earthen jars with long narrow necks were used for drinking water, which became cool if kept in a shady place with a good current of air. Everybody had one of these at the head of his bed on the roof, and how good that cold drink of water tasted the first thing on a summer morning!

Bread is the next necessity of life, after water. It is deeply respected by Arabs, and has a symbolic significance for them as the "provision of God." I have seen a small ragged boy take a piece of bread which someone had carelessly dropped on the ground, and kiss it reverently and murmur, "Rizk Allah!"

It is made of whole-wheat flour, sometimes mixed with barley by poor people for economy's sake, and is about the size and consistency of a large waffle. Many people get their bread from the public bakeries, but many others, like Om Fatima and my Hajjia, scorn any but home-baked bread. They had ovens in their kitchen courtyards, and so did most village dwellers. Morning and evening the smoke from the flaming *tanurs* was a familiar sight on the edge of town. A tanur is a round mud oven about three feet high, narrowed at the top and with an air outlet at the base. The inside is hollow and lined with fine clay. A fire of palm branches is lit inside and kept going furiously until the oven is hot. The breadmaker has been flapping the dough expertly from hand to hand to get it the right size, and as soon as the flames die down she inserts it deftly through the top and slaps it against the inner surface. Here it sticks until it is baked, and she knows the exact moment when it must be taken out.

Tea is another indispensable, for both rich and poor. For

breakfast it is often served with milk, but throughout the day clear tea, poured over sugar into narrow-waisted glasses called *istikans,* is the universal beverage. It is the color of horehound, and I have always imagined it tastes something like it. Poor Arabs regard sweet tea after a meal almost more important than the meal itself.

It is usually made in a samovar, which contains lighted charcoal and has a vertical flue through which the fumes escape. Around this heated center there is a container of water, with a small faucet to draw it off. Tea is made in a china teapot (imported from Czechoslovakia) and then placed on top of the flue of the samovar to steep, or put at the side of a brazier of charcoal.

My friends had beautiful brass samovars, which were kept polished till they shone like gold. A good working substitute for a brass one was made in the bazaar from flattened-out oil cans, and was just as efficient though not nearly so elegant.

Teas made from other plants than the usual one are common in Iraq, what the French call *tisanes.* Sometimes they are used because of their medicinal qualities, and often just because they are a refreshing change. My Hajjia used to have a special little fat teapot of *chai numi*—sour tea—a brew made of tiny lemons, dried and crushed, which are peculiar to Basrah. Politeness demands that one say "With pleasure" after a third glass of tea, meaning that you have had sufficient, but I have often said to her, "Hajjia, I am not going to say 'with pleasure' as long as there is any chai numi in the pot! I'm going to drink tea all the afternoon!"

The usages connected with the serving of coffee have an almost ritual significance to the Arabs, and have a whole set of traditions based on the ceremonial associated with hospitality. This is especially true in the desert, and tribal sheikhs have one special coffee maker, for whom the preparation of the beverage is a full-time job. He begins the day with the long and delicate process of roasting the coffee beans till they are exactly right. Then he proceeds to the equally long process of grinding the coffee in a mortar, and he finally makes it in one huge pot. When he has tasted it and made sure it is right, he decants it into the small shining coffeepots, like the large ones in shape, with fat bases and long pointed spouts.

Arab coffee is strong and rather bitter; it has no sugar, but is sometimes flavored with a little cardamom. It is served in small handleless cups, and is offered three times, unless the guest shakes his cup after the first round to show that no more is wanted. If you drink two cups, it is very rude not to drink a third. You might drink one just out of politeness, but if you drink two you can drink a third. It must never be taken with the left hand, nor must the empty cup ever be placed on the floor. For a guest to refuse coffee, or a host fail to offer it, can be a deadly insult and lead to grave consequences.

A story is told of a coffee expert from the Beni Temim tribe, who went to visit a sheikh of the Shammar. The servant who was passing the coffee noticed that the guest, whose headcloth was drawn across the lower part of his face, was pouring his coffee behind this kerchief instead of drinking it. When he was accused of this deception, he first denied it, for by the laws of hospitality he was bound to drink it once he had accepted it. Then he admitted that he had not been able to drink it because of something unpleasant about the aroma. A fresh brew was ordered, and the same thing happened. The sheikh was greatly perturbed about the purity of his coffee, and ordered the pot to be brought and poured out on a tray in front of them. Nothing was found, and he felt himself publicly insulted and was about to order that his unmannerly guest be killed. However, he gave the guest one more chance, and ordered that the large pot, from which the small one had been filled, be brought. This was emptied onto a large tray, and as the last of the fluid was being poured, a small spider dropped out.

"That," said the guest, "is the flavor I detected in the aroma of the coffee."

"By the Prophet!" exclaimed his host. "You shall have the title Connoisseur of Coffee, Class One! You detected a fault that none of the rest of us noticed. And for the rest of your life you need buy no more coffee, for we shall supply you with it as long as you live."

Turkish coffee is served in the towns, perhaps more than Arab coffee. This is sweet, with the sugar boiled in, and has froth on top when properly made. It is served in a tiny cup with a handle and its own saucer, and is offered only once.

A formal call is always concluded by the serving of coffee, and it is a serious breach of good manners to leave before it is passed. I was once kept waiting two hours in the house of an important family, who detained me by the simple means of not serving me coffee. I had gone to see Om Bedr on business, and her partner wife told me she would be returning home any minute. My mistake, of course, was in going in and sitting down, when I found that she was out; I should have said, "I'll come back tomorrow," and taken my leave. The sharp-tongued and somewhat jealous *sherika* had sherbet served to me, and she came and went, as did other members of the household. But no coffee was forthcoming and I didn't know the family well enough at that time to dare risk offending them by disregarding a well-known convention.

In large households, coffee was bought by the bag, tea by the chest, and rice, wheat, and sugar in large burlap sacks of several hundredweight each. Cooking fat—dihn—came in big tin drums. All these commodities would come into the courtyard on donkeys or camels. So did the tins of oil and the great sheaves of date branches used for fuel. Many bags of charcoal were needed for cooking, for samovars, and in winter for the braziers that were the chief means of heating the rooms. Later, oil heaters and oil cookstoves came into general use, and the ever-present primus stove, large and small. In my early years there was no electricity and everyone used oil lamps and lanterns.

Good housewives prepared many things at home. Tomato paste, called *ma'jun,* is made when tomatoes are plentiful and cheap. It is a long and complicated process and includes spreading them out on the roof, where the hot sun does the work, instead of a fire in a stove. The paste is used in soups, stews, and sauces throughout the year. *Bastarma* is a kind of hard sausage made of highly spiced mutton, and so similar to pastrami that I feel sure the two names have a common origin. This was one of Om Fatima's specialties; she felt she made and seasoned it a little better than anyone else. She used to send me two or three large ones every winter, and they would be hung from our kitchen rafters, like the hams and sides of bacon in our own country's pioneer days, and sliced off as we wanted it.

Delicious concentrated fruit juices, to make cooling drinks for summer, were prepared from oranges, limes, pomegranates, and mulberries.

My Hajjia made particularly excellent Arab pickles, and I happened to mention to her one day how John envied me when I described them, after I had been for one of my frequent meals with her.

"Well, he must have some too!" she exclaimed, and after that, every year when she made her supply, she sent a large jar to our house. The servant who brought them would always say with a grin, "These are for Abu John from the Hajjia—not for Om John!"

Everyone made a variety of jams from many delectable fruits as they came along. The most unusual to me was that made of *turinge,* a large citrus fruit with a rough pebbly skin. This was cut in long slices and preserved in syrup flavored with rose water and cardamom, and was especially good with buffalo cream and a big platter of fried eggs and fresh Arab bread—our usual breakfast when we went with the

Khazal boys down river to visit the Sheikh, their father, in spring vacations.

Arab ladies did not as a rule go to the bazaar very often. Om Fatima would sometimes put on a servant's abba and go on a tour of investigation, to check up on the prices of fruits and vegetables which were in season and make sure she wasn't being cheated by her servants. She would also take a quick look at the cloth bazaar, to see if the silk shops had anything new and striking from Bombay or Beirut that hadn't yet been sent around to the harems for inspection.

How glad I was that I was free to roam through the bazaars whenever I liked. No supermarket, however fabulous, can ever have the charm for me of those long aisles of open shops, with the high vaulted roofs, and the occasional shaft of sunlight from a high window in the ceiling cutting across the shade. The grocers' bazaar had the most fascinating compound of smells, with the spice shops, and the stalls with the baskets of lentils, rice of all kinds, dried peas and beans, grain, and nuts—walnuts, almonds, pistachio, hazelnuts, and melon seeds. Here were blue-green pottery bowls filled with tomato paste, for those who had run out of their homemade supply. Here were dried apricots packed in boxes, or pressed into long thin sheets looking like browny-orange oilcloth, to be used in making sherbet. Near them were dried pomegranate seeds, used to give certain meat dishes an astringent flavor.

Of course there were dates of every type and grade. Fancy ones packed for the export trade were in small tempting packages, and often stuffed with almonds or walnuts. Large boxes for family use contained pound packages, or were packed in bulk in long shining rows. At the other end of the scale were baskets of the poorer varieties of dates, or discards, which were sold as fodder for cows.

The spice and herb shops had the most to contribute to the blend of smells that was so intriguing. Arabia has for centuries been known as a land of spices, and was on the great trade routes that brought them from the East Indies by way of Ceylon and southern India up the Persian Gulf. Here they would be transhipped and taken by caravan all over the Near East. Herodotus says of spices: "The whole country is scented with them, and exhales an odor marvelously sweet."

I was astonished when I learned that there were at least forty different kinds of spices and herbs to be had in our bazaar. And how pleasant to see whole cloves and nutmegs, sticks of vanilla, and large pieces of cinnamon bark, instead of uniform rows of small cans, only varying in their labels.

The fruit bazaar was a delight to the eye as well as to the nose. Great piles of oranges, lemons, limes, turinges, and ruby-red pomegranates, bunches of bananas; and as the seasons progressed apricots, nectarines, peaches, plums, grapes, melons; and in the fall the plump golden ripe dates, described as "little bags of honey."

Here on a corner was an old man mending broken teapots and plates by "sewing" them—boring holes and putting in rivets; and opposite him a repairer of grindstones, laboriously chipping away at them.

The brass and copper bazaars were also a delight to the eye, but not to the ear, as the noise of the incessant pounding was deafening, and so was that of the tinsmiths' bazaar. Here they made every imaginable household utensil from the ubiquitous oil can.

Not far off was the section where quilts were made. The white cotton used for stuffing was fluffed up by a primitive whirring instrument with a taut string. We sent every year for the *neddaf* who did this work, to come to our back veranda and fluff up our roof mattresses for another season, a process which enchanted our children when they were small. Ordinary quilts were covered with bright red cotton cloth, but there were also silk- and satin-covered ones of every color of the rainbow. I was once visiting the family of an upcountry sheikh, in a settlement in the marshes outside Amarah, and was greatly taken by their arrangement to store quilts. At one end of a huge room there were tiers of open cupboards exactly like a pigeon cote, and in every pigeonhole a neatly rolled quilt of a different color. There must have been hundreds of them.

"These are for when we have guests," explained the hostess laconically.

The basket and matting bazaar was a beguiling place. Here everything was made either of reeds from the marshes, or from some part of the date palm. Great heavy mats for the walls of serifas, thinner and finer ones for the floor, round ones to serve meals on; baskets of every size and shape; rope; little covers to put on the top of water jars; and fans of every description. Our fans were always made for us in a special village, where the craftsmen (usually women) would weave in Arabic our names (many years later, my daughter and I were each given an OM JOHN one, as she is now Om John too) or GOOD MORNING, TO YOUR GOOD HEALTH, or WELCOME. Sometimes there would be a recognizable picture of a mosque, a sewing machine, or an airplane.

The goldsmiths' bazaar always reminded me of the Arabian Nights. Small, a little out of the way, the craftsmen there sat tranquilly behind their braziers with tiny blowpipes. On the low counters before them were little compartments full of unset turquoises, seed pearls, and what looked like rubies and emeralds. Delicately wrought filigree bracelets and necklaces and earrings were displayed; and there was a glass box of old gold coins. There was no sense of haste or urgency whatever. You felt they might easily have a pair of jeweled shoes behind the counter for Zubeidah, the consort of Caliph Haroun al Rashid, or be repairing one of the singing golden birds from the golden tree in her palace.

They were always ready to be obliging about unusual

jobs for ordinary mortals, too. I took them a fountain pen that had belonged to my mother: the working parts were not much good any more, but it had a beautiful gold case. They made me a bangle from it, which goes well with my others of Arab design, and the man who did it, and his fellow craftsmen, were all greatly interested in the project.

Nearby were shops full of beads, and Moslem rosaries of amber, mother-of-pearl, jet, agate, olivewood, and many other kinds, with the most entrancing assortment of tassels.

Little stationers had Arabic calendars and diaries, and amazing diagrams of the Ka'ba at Mecca; and the perfumer's tiny shop contained shelves full of small fancy embossed bottles of heavy sandalwood scent, attar of roses, and other potent perfumes.

Pigeons wheeled around the minaret of the great mosque at the entrance to the bazaars, and at its base were cages of squawking chickens waiting for purchasers.

The great blue dome towered above it all.

VIII

In the Name of God, the Compassionate, the Merciful

Fatima's baby son, as soon as he was born, had the Moslem call to prayer, the Azan, recited into his right ear:

> "God is Great!
> I testify that there is no God but God
> I testify that Mohammed is the Prophet of God
> Come to Prayer
> Come to good works
> God is great
> There is no God but God."

After this, his left ear received the Standing—a repetition of the Call to Prayer, prefaced by the words "We are standing up for Prayer."

When Hajji Izzat's old mother, Fatima's grandmother, was at the point of death, a Mullaya was in the room and read the chapter of the Koran called Ya Sin, which tradition says tranquilizes the departing soul. Everyone present recited the Moslem creed together, so the devout old lady passed into eternity with the name of God in her dying ears. It is the first and last word heard by every good Moslem, when they enter this world and when they leave it.

The Arab is an extremely religious person. The name of God is constantly on his lips, and the idea of God's omnipotence and man's submissiveness is deeply ingrained in his thought pattern and his emotions. The word Islam itself means "submission." From birth, every Moslem is indoctrinated with the fatalistic attitude that both good and evil are predestined. In spite of many inconsistencies in practical application, this attitude of mind colors human relationships, business dealings, and indeed all the affairs of life.

When I entered the Arab world, with my New England background of free will and personal responsibility, I would have found many situations completely incomprehensible, had I not known academically (and was soon to learn practically) that the fatalism of their religion was the key to behavior among Moslems. The tendency in Islam is to accept life and adjust to it, rather than to try to change it and mold it. "It is written" or "It is the will of God" is the inevitable attitude. In a world where all things are ordained by God, man has no ultimate control over events.

We read the Koran as part of our language course—some of it in Arabic, and all of it in an English translation—so I was familiar with the stately cadenced prose of the original, and learned its beauty and sublimity when intoned by a professional.

The Koran is the sacred book of Islam by which God revealed himself to man. The medium was the Prophet Mohammed, to whom God spoke at different times and under various circumstances, through the Angel Gabriel, over a period of twenty-three years. The messages were dictated and Mohammed transcribed them, on ribs of palm trees, tablets of white stone, and shoulder blades of sheep. Sometimes they were preserved in the memories of men.

I soon realized that Mohammed must not be considered to be the author of the Koran. He was merely God's passive instrument. Nor should one call his followers Mohammedans —they are Moslems. The Book—literally "The Reading"—is God's word and His only; every letter is sacred, and the Book, in meaning and letter alike, is divinely inspired.

My Arab friends made it abundantly clear to me how deeply they reverenced each individual copy of their holy book. It might never be touched with unwashed hands, never be held below the waistline, and never, never be laid on the floor. It was never carried about exposed to dust or to irreverent handling, but always was wrapped in a fine silk handkerchief, or a piece of clean cloth, preferably white. The little boys in the mosque school, gabbling their lessons by rote, had each a little reading desk to hold his Koran well above his lap.

Moslems preferred not to have non-Moslems touch their Book. I wanted, some years ago, to get a copy of the Koran to send as a gift to a friend in America, and I asked one of John's teachers to buy it for me in Zobeir. He handed it over to me in private, and no one knew of the transaction.

Just before I left Basrah for the last time, I was choosing small, typically Arab articles in the old bazaar, to take to America as presents—tea glasses; tiny coffee cups; coarse wooden combs such as Bedu women use; gay glass bangles; and a good supply of seven-eye beads. I selected quite a few strings of what are called "conversation beads"—used more to play with than to pray with. The minute shop where I found them had all sorts of rosaries hanging up in fascinating profusion, and as I was looking over the bright tassels I spied some miniature Korans in little metal cases.

"Hajji," I said to the old man who kept the shop, "I would like a few of those." I was emboldened to ask for them, as I had known him for years and his grandsons had been in our school. He sold them to me without any comment, and when

I got home I wished I had bought more. So I went back next day, but he had gone to the mosque to pray and a friend was minding the shop. This man flatly refused to sell me any Korans. I didn't argue, because I knew I was lucky to have got any at all. As I was turning away, the Hajji came back.

"What can I do for you, Khanum?" he asked hospitably. (Some old-fashioned people like to continue to use this title for a lady, which had been common in Turkish days.)

I made my request rather timidly, and he said to his friend, "Of course she may have them. She and her late husband are People of the Book."

The Koran consists of one hundred and fourteen chapters of varying length called Surahs. Some are as short as the Lord's Prayer, and others as long as the Book of Genesis. They emphasize the unity of God, His attributes, the religious duties of man, and ultimate retribution and reward. They also lay down detailed regulations for prayer, fasting, pilgrimage, and almsgiving. In them is the pronouncement forbidding wine, pork, and gambling; and they regulate marriage, divorce and inheritance, as well as the treatment of slaves.

The Koran is considered to be the basis of all theology and jurisprudence, and its study constitutes the major part of the curriculum wherever religious leaders are trained.

A body of literature called the Traditions is second only to the Koran in authority. After the Prophet's death, whenever a precedent was needed, a case would be quoted telling what he had done in similar circumstances. To make this authentic, the links in the chain of transmission had to be cited—A had it from B, who had it from C, who had it from D, that the Prophet (upon him be peace!) did so-and-so. This record of all the sayings and doings of Mohammed was called the Sunna—the Path, or Way—and those who accepted the six authentic books of the Traditions came to be known as Sunnis, those of the Path. They also acknowledged the first

four Khalifahs (the leaders of Islam after the Prophet) as
rightful successors of Mohammed.

The other great sect of Islam, the Shiahs—which means
"Followers"—do not accept the Sunna or Six Traditions,
but have five of their own. Their basic disagreement with
the Sunnis was on the question of Mohammed's successors.
They maintain it should have been the stock of the Prophet
who ruled after him, beginning with his son-in-law Ali,
whom they follow.

There are endless sects and subsects in Islam, as there are
in Christianity, and it took me years even to begin to sort
them out.

One year, when my old Zahra and I were arranging for our
annual distribution of garments to very poor people, I said to
her, "Zahra, why is it that we never seem to know any people
from Firsi, that little village next to Abbas, on the way in
to Basrah City? We have people from almost every other
village along Ashar Creek. We have no club girls from Firsi
and you never take me there."

Zahra assumed her most impressive and mysterious expression.

"Om John, they are not the sort of people you would care
to know."

"I care to know everybody!" I said impatiently. "Why
don't they want to know *us?*"

She then gave me a quick sketch of the Sheikhites, or
Sheikhlis, as they were variously called—why they lived so
separate from their neighbors, and what their special peculi-
arities were. They had a strict and detailed ritual about the
most intimate physical functions, which they considered part
of their religious obligations. Long before Zahra was through
I winced and said feebly to her, "That's enough!" but she
was relentless. "You said you wanted to know, so I'm telling
you!" When she had finished the last graphic detail, she
concluded triumphantly, "*Now* do you see why I said they

weren't the kind of people you would like to know?"

Fatima's family were Sunni, and I learned a great deal about that branch of the Believers from her aunt. Hajjia Sudika had gone on the pilgrimage to Mecca with her parents and her brother as a young girl. Her marriage was childless, and when her husband died she returned to the family home as a matter of course, and thereafter occupied herself chiefly with religion.

Islam as a system requires Faith, *Iman,* what you believe; and Practice, *Din,* which is what you do.

Belief in God is the first and most important article of faith. He is omniscient and omnipotent; He wills all things, good and evil—even the wills of men. He sees all things, even the steps of a black ant on a black stone on a black night.

To God are given ninety-nine beautiful names, or attributes, many of which occur in the Koran, and which are frequently used as men's names, prefixed by Abdul, which means "the servant of"—the Mighty One, the Glorious, the Merciful, the Forgiving.

Fatima's Aunt Sudika showed me the lovely amber rosary which had belonged to her husband—ninety-nine clear perfect beads, in groups of thirty-three each, held together by the long pointer, or "minaret" bead, with its tassel. This was sometimes called the Imam, after the prayer leader in a mosque.

"See, Om John," said Sudika to me. "Every bead is a name of God, and the pointer is the Great Name of God. No mortal knows it!" she said solemnly. "Solomon is said to have known it, and could tell the jinn to do his bidding. Some frivolous people say that the camel knows it, and will not tell. That is why he looks so supercilious!"

Sudika used the rosary always for her prayers.

The second article of Faith is Belief in God's Angels. These are Gabriel, God's messenger and the medium of revelation; Azrael, the Angel of Death, who comes to man at his last hour and receives his soul; Azrafel, who will sound the last trumpet at the Resurrection; and Michael, in whose care is the sustenance of all created beings and who is the special protector of the Jews.

After God's Angels came God's Books.

"You know, Om John," Sudika used to say earnestly, "you Christians are People of the Book, too! God sent over one hundred of his books to the children of men, and all are lost except four. To Moses the Pentateuch was revealed, to David the Psalms, to Jesus the Gospel, and to Mohammed the Koran."

She also instructed me about God's prophets. Twenty-five are mentioned by name in the Koran.

"But the ones on whom we must believe," she said, "are Adam, the chosen of God; Noah, the prophet of God; Abraham, the friend of God; Moses, the spokesman, who conversed with God; Jesus, the spirit of God, or the word of God; and Mohammed, the messenger of God. Upon him be peace!" she concluded.

The Resurrection and the Last Day, and the Predestination of Good and Evil, completed the list of prescribed beliefs.

I was used to hearing "It is Fate"—"Kismet," or "Naseeb"—in almost every conversation; and "In sha'Allah"—"God willing"—in practically every sentence.

"All that has been, or that will be," said my devout Arab friend, "was decreed in eternity and was written on the Preserved Tables."

This was a tablet called Louh Mahfuz, upon which the actions of men and the Koran were recorded before creation, according to the teaching of Mohammed.

These beliefs are obligatory on Sunni Moslems and Shiahs alike, and so is Practice, or Din, which is composed of the Five Pillars.

The first is repetition of the Creed: "I testify that there is no God but God, and Mohammed is the Apostle of God."

This has been the battle cry of Moslem armies everywhere, and is uttered daily by two hundred and fifty million believers. The national flag of Saudi Arabia bears the inscription, in white on a green ground, *There is no God but God.* I shall never forget how incongruous this looked to me the first time I saw it on the license plate of a transdesert truck, but I became accustomed to it.

The second Pillar is Prayer. This must be performed five times daily—at dawn, noon, midafternoon, sunset, and two hours after sunset. When I first went to Basrah all clocks and watches were kept by Arab time, when sunset was twelve o'clock. This made it easy to calculate the time for prayer, and it was convenient to know how much daylight was left. But it was very bad indeed for the works of our timepieces, which had to be changed every day. It also led to endless confusion as to which day was which, for Friday eve was Thursday night, and Saturday eve was Friday night, and so on, and the possibility of misunderstandings was infinite. I have arrived at a place on the wrong evening, and worse still have had a whole group of Arab ladies come to my house twenty-four hours before I expected them. We kept one set of clocks and watches with Arabic time; and we had comparative calendars which showed us how the days of the lunar month corresponded to our Western reckonings.

In those first years we ran our schools by Arab time, of course, and it took me a long while after European time had become universal to get used to the idea that half past three was not the normal time to call the roll in the morning, and half past six the hour for the noon recess to begin.

For prayer, the worshiper has to be ceremonially clean and must face Mecca. Travelers often carried a pocket compass which was called a "Mecca pointer." The necessary ablutions are to wash the face in clean water, the arms above the elbow, the hands, and the feet.

It is taken for granted that the ceremonial cleansing of the private parts has already been performed—for a man, after intercourse or nocturnal emission; and for women after menstruation, intercourse, and childbirth. Clean sand is permissible if water is lacking. Both men's and women's garments used to be made with long slits in the sleeves, so that they could be pushed up for the ceremonial ablutions.

After purification came posture, with every stage precisely prescribed, as were the phrases to be uttered.

It was a common sight on the fashionable At Home days for ladies, to see one of the older guests rise and step out of the room, request a prayer carpet from a servant outside, and retire to another apartment. Here she would swathe her neck, head and shoulders in a special white scarf, and then perform the rite of afternoon prayer.

I was always prepared to offer to my Hajjia, or Fatima's aunt, or my strict friend Om Ibrahim, a bedroom to which they could retire, whenever these families came to have afternoon tea with me.

The Call to Prayer is given by a Mueddin from the top of the minaret of a mosque, and blind men were usually chosen for this office, so that they could not look down into nearby courtyards and see the women.

Fasting is the third Pillar. Ramadhan is the tenth month of the lunar year, and toward the end is the Night of Power, when the Koran came down entire to the lowest heaven, from whence it was revealed in portions by Gabriel, as the occasion required.

"How many Moslems really fast, Sudika?" I asked her in my early days. I knew that young children and the mentally defective were exempt, and that sick people and those on a journey of more than three days were excused, but had to make it up eventually.

"Everyone!" she said firmly. "Of course you know that women who are pregnant are excused, and those who are nursing a child. One may not fast at her time of the month, and so we are always left with a debt to make up afterward."

I happened to know that some of my husband's men friends did not fast, but I prudently did not argue the point with her.

If I had asked her the question thirty years later, she could not have answered it so categorically. It is impossible now to estimate how many do or don't fast, but certainly the prestige and importance of the principle has as firm a hold on the Moslem world as it ever did. I have heard broadcasts from Cairo on the spiritual benefits of the fast, the psychological benefits, and the physical benefits. Religion and nationalism are closely interwoven and it is a demonstration of loyalty as well as piety to observe this Pillar.

The fast-breaking holiday, the Eed el Fitur, at the end of Ramadhan, is a three-day period after the new moon has been seen by reliable witnesses, and everyone rejoices at the completion of the fast. All who can afford it have new clothes; calls are paid; and swings, merry-go-rounds, and little Ferris wheels are erected in every vacant space. Donkeys are beautified with patterns of henna and fancy harness, and cheap rides are one of the great treats for children. Every sort of vehicle is brought out and gaily decorated and pressed into service. A general holiday spirit prevails, and the social side of the festival is emphasized rather than the religious one.

The fourth Pillar of Religion is Almsgiving. There are legal alms, requiring one fortieth of the income, or two and one half per cent. Then there are also free-will offerings. Beggars feel that they are conferring a favor on the faithful, by helping them to earn merit with God, when they call the attention of the passers-by to their begging bowls. Soup kitchens, with a free meal for every comer, are often set up by wealthy people every night during the month of Ramadhan. Large meals for the poor are often cooked and distributed after a death in a well-to-do family or in fulfillment of a vow.

"Fatima, I just don't understand it," I said to her once.

"This whole idea of 'earning merit,' as though God were a bank and you must keep up your credit with him lest you get 'in the red.' You really do these things to relieve human suffering and want, don't you?"

"God has decreed it so!" was her invariable answer. "He is the Merciful One!"

The Pilgrimage to Mecca is the fifth and last Pillar. It is performed in Dhu el Hajj, the last month of the lunar year, and is completed on the tenth day of that month. How I used to enjoy hearing my Hajjia and her sister, and their venerable mother when she was alive, relate their experiences when the whole family went on the pilgrimage in an early year of the century. Those were the days when the entire journey from Basrah was made by ship and took a month or more. The pilgrim ship they traveled on must have been quite de luxe, for they had two cabins, and a good-sized space on deck, curtained off for privacy. They took all their own provisions with them, complete with several crates of live chickens, and a goat to provide them with fresh milk.

"We often had fresh meat," put in the old Hajjia. "There was a butcher on the ship, with plenty of live sheep which he kept down below, and every few days he would slaughter one, and we could all buy a portion."

They landed at Mother Eve's town, the seaport of Jidda, and from there traveled by camel up to Mecca.

"When we got there," related my friends, "we had to leave off our own clothes and put on pilgrims' garb. It was wonderful! Everyone equal with everyone else, before God! Then for ten days we went back and forth and round and round. We encircled the Kaaba, we kissed the Black Stone, we stoned the Devil, and we drank of the well Zem-zem. You know that is the well from which Abraham's wife Hagar and her son Ishmael drank in the wilderness."

The old Hajjia asked me with a chuckle, "Did you know that over there they call a thermos bottle a Zemzemiya?"

"We made many prayers," continued her daughter, "and listened to many sermons. Then, on the tenth day, the great Day of the Sacrifice, my father had a sheep sacrificed for each one of us. After that he and my brothers had their heads shaved, everyone had his nails pared, and we put on our regular clothes again. Each of us was given a certificate to show that we had performed the Hajj."

I was always pleased when my annual visit to Kuwait coincided with the preparations for people going from there on the pilgrimage. They usually went overland, by caravan, and the camel bazaars there and in Zobeir were hives of industry. Camel saddles, brightly colored harness and saddlebags, and litters for the women, called *kajawahs,* were all made ready for the great exodus across the desert. Tents, bedding, fodder for the animals as well as all the food supplies for the human beings, cooking pots and fuel, all had to be carefully organized.

The whole pilgrimage was a much more lengthy and complicated affair in those days than now, when most people go by plane; though there are still many contractors who arrange transportation for those who prefer cars and buses.

The pilgrimage to Mecca is incumbent on every Moslem, man or woman, who can pay his own expenses and provide for his dependents at home during his absence. A person who is incapacitated may pay the expenses of a substitute and get the credit himself. A woman must be accompanied by a husband or a male relative. I had one enterprising friend who lacked a male escort, so she married in order to have a lawful protector for the expedition, and after they returned home divorced him amicably by mutual consent.

The Feast of the Sacrifice, the tenth day of the month, is one of the two great festivals of Moslems the world over. The religious nature of this one is stressed much more than the Eed el Fitur at the end of Ramadhan, though it is celebrated in much the same way. Every family who can afford it sacrifices a sheep, and the tradition is said to go back to the days of Abraham. I have heard a legend that the Milky Way is the path in the sky of the Heavenly Ram which God sent to be sacrificed in the place of Isaac.

Boys and girls with the name Mekki or Mekkia have presumably been born or conceived at Mecca.

But I soon found that for Shiahs, pilgrimages to the Holy Cities of Iraq are no less imperative than the one to Mecca. The graves of the Imams, and especially the tomb of the martyred grandson of the prophet, Hussein, are sacred spots. Pious Shiahs will save up for years, and poor people will often sell literally everything that they possess, in order to go to Kerbala and Nejf. The Shiah pilgrim may even be provided with a temporary wife, legal as long as the arrangement lasts, and whose children, if she has any, are reared and educated by the religious foundations.

It is considered a great blessing to die in one of the Holy Cities, so age and infirmity prevent no one from undertaking the journey: the great thing is to get there in time to draw the last breath. The next best thing is to be taken there for burial, and many devout Shiahs provide in their wills that their remains shall be conveyed thither for interment, that they may acquire this special merit, and be found in holy ground at the day of resurrection. The transportation of coffins is a flourishing business, and the price paid for a grave depends upon its nearness to the principal shrine at Kerbala or Nejf. There is an official organization in which both Customs and the Health Department are concerned. The Customs collects a small duty, and examines the body to prevent smuggling of contraband, and the Health Department has to be on the watch for contagious diseases and epidemics. Most of the bodies sent to Iraq for burial are classified as "dry"; that is, desiccated as the result of previous burial; they are quite light and a dozen or so can be tied lengthwise on a donkey. The number of "wet" corpses is not so numerous,

[130]

and are usually those of people of wealth or position whose heirs arrange for burial at once. One such funeral was carried by airplane from Syria to Nejf in midsummer.

My Hajjia and her family were Shiahs and from them I learned a good deal about the special observances and prejudices of this sect. But most of all I got from a really great woman to whom they introduced me, the famous Mullaya Medina. She was the outstanding religious leader among all the Shiah women of the region, and I counted it a privilege to become her intimate friend. She respected me because my life, like hers, had religious motivation, and we had real spiritual companionship. She was a profound mystic, and her vivid perception of the life of the spirit was stimulating and inspiring. She deeply regretted the fact that I was, from her point of view, a *kafir*—literally "one who hides or covers up the truth." It is used to define anyone who does not believe in the ministry of the Prophet Mohammed and his Koran.

"Oh, Om John!" she exclaimed to me one of the last times I ever talked to her. "You and I are such friends, we agree on so many things, what a pity that we cannot be together in eternity! But you are a kafir and you will go to hell!"

She it was who first showed me a *torbat* and told me what it is used for. It is a small piece of baked clay about two inches in length, round or oblong, and the manufacture of these torbats is one of the industries of Kerbala.

"See, Om John," she said. "Here is the name of Ali and of Fatima, upon them be peace. These are made of holy earth, and he who rests his forehead upon one of these during his prayer prostrations is praying on sacred ground!"

Mullaya Medina had twice performed the pilgrimage to Mecca, and been many times to the holy cities of Iraq. She told me once that she wished she could go to Mecca every year. She found it a tremendous spiritual experience.

It was in the black-draped courtyard, or *Ma'atam*, where

the Mullaya carried on her readings in the month of Moharram, that I had my first personal experience of this great
landmark in the Shiah Moslem year.

The month of Moharram (literally "forbidden"), the first
month of the lunar year, is as important to the Shiah part of
Islam as Dhu el Hajj or Ramadhan. The Sunnis agree that
the tenth day of this month was when Adam and Eve were
created, likewise heaven and hell and the Tablet of Decree,
but they have no part whatever in the Ashur celebrations of
the first ten days, so intensely significant to the Shiahs.

While the Sunnis regard Abu Bakr, Omar, Othman and
Ali as the lawful first four Khalifs, the Shiahs believe that
Ali was the first lawful Khalif (or Iman), and regard the
other three as usurpers. They are particularly bitter against
Omar, whose name is anathema and whom they seek to be-
little and defame on every possible occasion.

The tragedy of Kerbala is enacted every year. The story
is as follows:

Ali, the fourth Khalif (literally successor) and Imam, noted
for his holiness and saintliness, was praying in the mosque
at Kufa, near Baghdad, when he was mortally wounded by
an assassin and escaped on a camel. His supposed grave is
the center of the shrine at Nejf. After his death, his successors proved unworthy and the people of Kufa sent to
Mecca for Ali's son Hussein, whose mother was the Prophet's
daughter Fatima. They pledged their support if he would
come and seize the Khalifate again for the "holy family."
However, the promised forces failed to appear when Hussein
and his little band met the enemy on the plain of Kerbala,
their numbers were reduced by slaughter and thirst, and first
Hussein's young son and then he himself were killed and carried off.

The Battle of Kerbala is annually commemorated in the
Moharram Passion Play, and the small early cult of Ali has
grown into a great cult of Ali and Hussein. For ten days,

readings go on in the mosques or in specially prepared gathering places hung with black and called *Ma'atams,* coming to a great climax on the eve of the tenth day, which is Ashur.

A procession is formed on the great night, headed by men who are religious leaders, and carefully regulated by police. They are followed by bands of breast beaters, flagellants or chainmen, and head cutters, and dramatic representations of the actual tragedy itself. Swinging lights are carried to symbolize the lights in the camp of the host at Kerbala, followed by riderless camels accompanied by crowds shouting in grief over the loss of their leaders, a small child on a led horse impersonating the young son of Hussein, and a grisly dummy representing the headless and bleeding corpse of Hussein himself.

I used to watch this procession with breathless interest every Moharram, sitting with women friends in a second-story window overlooking the line of march.

But I had been in Basrah for several years, and had come to know Mullaya Medina well, before I went to any of the women's own observances. She asked me if I wouldn't like to attend a Moharram reading.

"I would love to, Mullaya," I told her eagerly. "But I am afraid that some of the women might think I was watching out of curiosity, and would resent my presence."

"No indeed!" she replied emphatically. "Everyone knows you, and that you have a regard for all religion. In any case" —grandly—"if I ask you to come, that is enough."

Accordingly, I came with a young pupil of the Mullaya's, who was one of her corps of assistant readers. She settled me with friends in the front row of an upstairs veranda overlooking the courtyard. This was now black-draped and had become a Ma'atam, with a huge towering throne covered in black which was both the leader's seat and the pulpit.

Women were streaming in, children of every age were

running around, and everyone, even to the smallest baby in arms, was dressed in mourning. The pupils and satellites of the Mullaya at long last gathered themselves into a circle at the foot of the pulpit and began to untie the wrappings from their holy books. Last of all, Mullaya Medina herself made a sweeping and striking entrance, climbed the steps of the *mumbar* (the pulpit), seated herself, and a hush fell upon the assembly.

She was a woman with great eloquence and dramatic power, and she swayed her audience to tears, sobs, and groans, and back to breathless attention while they hung on every word. The tension mounted and worked up at the end to the rhythmic chanting, wailing, shrieking, and ritual breast beating which concludes every session.

I had read Sir Lewis Pelly's classic translation of the Passion Play and knew what the story was. I went every day of the ten days that year, my first Ashur, and by reading the Pelly translation for the day each morning before I went, I could follow the details of the story. I was considered very knowledgeable by the women sitting near me!

That year Moharram was in summer and it was very hot. I took a good supply of my husband's large handkerchiefs with me, to wipe my streaming face when the perspiration ran down into my eyes. I likewise, when the women were all chanting and beating their breasts, occasionally patted my knee, involuntarily, in time to the rhythm. (And I defy anyone, sitting in that atmosphere, not to be caught up in the spirit of it, and keep time.) Next day, the teachers in John's school told him that they had heard in the bazaar that Mrs. Van Ess had been greatly affected by the Ashur reading, and had cried a great deal!

Every year after that, as long as Mullaya Medina lived, I used to go to some of the readings, although I never again followed them all through. Women find in these gatherings a social satisfaction, dramatic gratification, and emotional release, all bound up with religious fervor. Ashur was the high spot, but the readings were continued in a lower emotional tone all through Moharram and the following month of Sefr, and all good Shiahs wore black for the whole two months.

Sunni women had large gatherings for special occasions called Mauluds, when they had specially trained musicians perform the famous Birth Song of the Prophet. This is a classic which has come down through Moslem history, and is rendered with an accompaniment of drums, cymbals, and chanting. The occasion may be to offer thanks for recovery from illness, safe return of some member of the family from a journey, the circumcision of a small boy, or in fulfillment of a vow.

Moslem women seldom if ever went to the mosques in Basrah. Although the founders of the religion never intended that women should be debarred from public worship, the tendency of men was to wish to keep their wives and daughters from observance. This led in some countries to women not going to the mosques at all. In the countries where they do so, they are usually in a secluded corner, so that feminine proximity may not distract the male worshipers from their devotions.

IX

The Dark Angel

Azrael, the Angel of Death, is an expected and familiar figure to all believers. As Fatima said to me so philosophically, "Everyone is born and everyone dies." The great thing is to die with the name of God on one's lips.

"Oh, Om John," she said to me after her old grandmother, the Bibi, had died, "I was so glad they didn't pour water on my Bibi's face and into her mouth when she lay dying! They had some ready, brought from the well Zem-zem at Mecca, but she realized that we were all repeating the Witness, and her lips moved so that we knew she was joining in it. God is generous!"

She went on. "Sometimes they pour so much water on the dying person's face that he nearly chokes! Some people pour sherbet—just sugar and water—into his mouth. This is to help the departure of the soul. And I have heard"—this in a low voice—"that there are people who strike or pull the person who is at the point of death, to make him give his own Witness!"

It was from my old Zahra that I learned most about the procedure after death. She was an expert at preparing bodies for burial and was often called on to perform this service.

As soon as life is extinct, and women have begun the loud wailing which is the sign of a death, the limbs of the dead person are straightened out and the two big toes tied together.

"You know, Om John," said Zahra impressively, "when people meet and greet each other, they are supposed to stand with their feet side by side so that the toes are in a straight line. When the departed one meets his Lord, must his feet not be in the correct position? This is why we tie the great toes together."

The haste with which funerals take place was a shock to me when I first lived in the Moslem world. Not only is the body prepared for burial as soon as possible, but the pall-bearers carry the coffin to the cemetery at what looks to un-accustomed eyes like a quick trot.

"It is not proper to keep a dead body in the house," asserted Zahra. "The Prophet, upon him be peace, said that if the departed is a good man, the sooner he is buried the more quickly he will reach heaven. If he is bad, he should be speed-ily buried, so that his unhappy lot may not fall upon others in the house. As long as the corpse is in the house, the rela-tives will go on weeping and will not eat. This is not good."

Moslems do not like funerals after sunset. In Bahrain they aver that the cemetery would say, of an evening interment, "It is my dinner," and would then demand a corpse every night.

There is a general washing place for the dead adjoining every mosque, but except in times of an epidemic, it is per-mitted to prepare the body for burial at home, provided the deceased died in his own house. A hole used to be dug in the earth to receive the water used in the washing, as it would be bad to tread on this water spread over a large area. Wash-ing the body is very important, as it must be thoroughly puri-fied and made presentable for the interviews that await it.

"The dead must be laid with the head to the east for the

washing," said Zahra. "And the feet to the west. We wash the body with soap and clean it well of all earthly filth. The nostrils and mouth are cleansed with wicks of cloth or cotton, gently, because the life has only just departed. Then we perform the prayer ablutions for the person, as in life; then throw camphor water from a new pot, three times—once from head to feet, then from right shoulder to feet, and then from the left—and each time we repeat the Word of Witness."

After this, the body is perfumed. Here there is great variation between different sects and localities. Spicy herbs, incense, and different powders are used, according to the means and taste of the survivors. Then comes the very important matter of the shroud. This is considered to be the covering in the next world, and must be without spot or blemish, and white, according to the decree of the Prophet. The outside covering is a winding sheet, long enough to be tied at both ends. The Shiahs untie this after the corpse has been placed in position in the grave so that it can move about to pray. They used to put a rosary under the head, and a torbat of earth from holy Kerbala near to the hand. Two date branches, one on each side of the corpse, were to serve as crutches for the dead when they got up to pray. Sand was put into the mouth of the corpse, as a confession that it was made of dust and to dust it must return.

Every mosque has biers which may be used by anyone to convey a corpse to the cemetery. As a rule, a coffin is used only if it is to be taken a long way, involving a train journey, or one by camel back or donkey. It is an act of merit to help carry a coffin or bier even a few paces, as well as a token of respect for the dead, and many men will crowd up to put a shoulder under the bier as it is being taken quickly along. Among some Moslems there is a tradition that no one should precede the corpse because the angels go before. As they hurry along, the bearers chant, "There is no God but God."

Prayers are read in the mosque, and then again just outside the cemetery. The graveyard is too polluted a place to hold the sacred office. Someone present calls out, "Here begin the prayers for the dead." The men present then arrange themselves in rows—three, five, or seven (it must be an uneven number)—with their faces toward Mecca. The Imam stands opposite, and when everyone is in place recites: "I purpose to perform prayers to God for this dead person, consisting of four Takbirs." (A Takbir is the statement that God is great.)

He puts his hands to the lobes of his ears and says the first Takbir.

"God is great!"

Then he folds his hands, the right over the left, and recites:

"Holiness to Thee, O God,
And to Thee be praise.
Great is Thy Name.
Great is Thy Greatness
Great is Thy Praise
There is no deity but Thee."

Then the second Takbir:

"God is Great!"

followed by:

"O God, have mercy on Mohammed and upon his descendants, as Thou didst bestow mercy, and peace, and blessing, and compassion and great kindness upon Abraham and upon his descendants.

"Thou art praised, and Thou art great!"

After some repetition, the third Takbir follows:

"God is great!

"Oh God, forgive our living and our dead and those of us who are present, and those who are absent, and our children, and our full-grown persons, our men and our women. O God, those whom Thou dost keep alive amongst us, keep alive in Islam, and those whom Thou causest to die, let them die in the Faith."

Then is the fourth Takbir:

"God is Great!"

The Iman turns his head to the right and says:

"Peace and mercy be to Thee,"

and then repeats it with his head to the left.

The Takbir is recited aloud by the Imam, but in the prayers which follow it, the people join in a low voice.

After this, those present seat themselves on the ground and raise their hands in silent prayer for the deceased's soul, and then they say to the relatives, "It is the decree of God," and the chief mourner responds, "I am pleased with the will of God."

As the corpse is placed in the grave, those who put it there say, "We commit thee to earth in the name of God and in the religion of the Prophet."

In many places v. 57 of the xxth Surah of the Koran is recited as clods of earth are thrown into the grave:

"From it [the earth] have We [God] created you, and unto it will We return you, and out of it will We bring you forth the second time."

This is objected to by the Wahabis—the Puritans of Islam —and by some learned divines.

A recess has been made at the side, on the bottom of the grave, to receive the corpse, whose face is toward Mecca; and the bands of the shroud are loosed so that the dead person can sit up to pray and to be interviewed by the angels.

After the burial, the people offer a Fatihah (the first chapter of the Koran) in the name of the deceased, and again when they have proceeded about forty paces from the grave.

"You know, Om John," Zahra told me, "in some places, the Shiahs instruct the dead person before they cover over the grave completely. The Mullah bends down and says, 'O So-and-So, when the interviewing angels come, say: God is my God, Mohammed is my prophet, Ali is my redeemer, The Koran is my book and Mecca is my Kibla. [The Kibla means the place to which one turns when praying.] And then, the moment the Mullah has repeated it all in the name of the dead person, they slap a handful of plaster over the opening, so to keep the testimony in the grave!"

She went on to say that when it was completely filled in and the "stones of testimony" in place at the head and foot, water is poured over the grave to cool the departed spirit, and for the bearers, who gather around the grave while the ground is wet, so that they may put their fingers in the mud and say prayers for the dead.

"And then," she concluded, "they have dates and sweets and bread, and go home!"

But the departure of the mourners is not the end for the one who has just been buried. As soon as the living have gone their forty paces away, the dead person is visited by two black angels with blue eyes, named Munkar and Nakir. The Shiahs say that they first smell of his feet, and if on them is the smell of sacred soil, there is no further examination. But if the feet have not gone on a pilgrimage, every member of the body is questioned separately as to what it has done or not done, to see whether the laws of Islam have been observed. If the answers are satisfactory he will be allowed to sleep in peace. But if not, he will be struck with an iron hammer and will roar so loudly that he will be heard by all who are anywhere near his grave.

"And, Om John," said Zahra solemnly, "on the Resurrection morning, the souls are all taken out of heaven, and God makes them walk the straight way which is as narrow as a hair, and is the bridge between heaven and hell. Those whose good deeds exceed their evil ones will pass over safely, and those whose deeds have been evil will fall off into hell-fire!"

Food is cooked and distributed to the poor for several days after a death, according to the resources of a family, and again at the fortieth day. Readings are held in the homes, as a memorial and to say prayers for the dead. Sunni Moslems do not have nearly as many funeral ceremonies as Shiahs, either at the funeral or afterward; and Sunni women are much more quiet and restrained in their mourning. Shiah readings for the women, after a death, usually end in the same sort of emotional crisis as the Moharram gatherings, when Hussein is bewailed, and everyone is exhausted by the abandon of sobbing and crying.

A universal custom among Moslems is for the bereaved family to be visited by their friends for at least three days after a death. A room or courtyard is arranged with nothing but floor coverings and cushions around the wall. The mourners sit at one side, their abbas over their heads, to be drawn across their faces if they are overcome by emotion or do not wish to be stared at. There is always a Mullaya present—several, if the family is well-to-do—to read and chant from time to time. Friends and neighbors come and go; some merely pay their respects, sit a short time, and then depart, bowing to the mourners and touching their hands, with a murmured formula of sympathy. Others stay the whole forenoon, or the entire day. At no time is a sorrowing woman left alone unless she wishes to withdraw, when it is perfectly permissible to do so. She is not obliged to make conversation, nor reply to well-intentioned but tactless remarks. Her grief is not intruded upon, but she is surrounded by human companionship and sympathy as she silently begins to make the tremendous psychological and spiritual adjustments of bereavement. There are always relatives and neighbors who take charge of the household, seeing that meals are cooked for any number of people, and that the supply of coffee never runs out, as this must be served to all who come to pay their condolences.

When one of Fatima's sons died, a promising young officer in the Air Force who was killed in a plane crash, I went and sat in her courtyard for a whole forenoon. The Mullayas chanted beautifully and impressively, and all our friends were there. When I left, I went across to where Fatima was sitting, touched her hand, and kissed her shoulder. No words passed between us, but she lifted her face and gave me an anguished look, and unspoken communication flowed from each of us to the other.

I have always felt that this whole custom was psychologically very sound. In a modified form, I observed it when my husband died, only a few days before we were to have left Basrah for retirement. In place of Mullayas I had several of the older women of the Arab Evangelical Church, my close friends of many years, who read suitable passages from the Psalms and the New Testament, and some of the beautiful Arabic Christian prayers appropriate to the occasion. It was an inexpressible comfort to me to see so many of my Arab friends, without any of the strain of having to take part in conversation, and they appreciated the opportunity to show me their love and sympathy.

A Moslem widow must observe four months and ten days of strict mourning. Enlightened and progressive families, Sunni as well as Shiah, revert to traditional customs at the great crises of life. One of my friends, a young woman who was well educated, cultured, and of broad interests, was suddenly left a widow before she was thirty, with four young children. She saw no one but her parents and sisters—none of the women friends who came to condole with her. She remained in this seclusion during the whole period of formal mourning. I went again, after the official readings were over, but her mother explained to me, in some distress, that Nuria intended to carry out the strictest seclusion and would see no one till the time had elapsed.

"You know, Om John," explained Om Nuria, "she may not have the moon shine on her, because that is masculine in

Arabic grammar. She mustn't be seen by a cock, a male dog or cat, or even a male flea or ant!"

I forebore from pressing the query, which I was tempted to make, of how she would go about it to distinguish between male and female ants and fleas.

Nuria's mother very wisely took her on the pilgrimage to Mecca the following year, accompanied by an elderly uncle. They visited Egypt and Syria as well as the holy cities of Islam, and she greatly benefited by her travels. She regained her perspective and on her return home threw herself energetically into the task of making a home for her children, and seeing that they had the best possible education. She was much more religious than she had been before she was widowed, but Nuria made a creative use of her experience.

Another very good friend of mine lost her favorite son in a motor accident. She retired to her country house, dressed in such deep mourning that she looked like a nun, and stayed completely within the house. She didn't even go up on the roof to sleep in the hot weather. I used to go to see her often and we had many long talks. Her spiritual perceptions were greatly sharpened by the experience, but she developed some of the characteristics of a recluse and a mystic. This was very hard on her surviving children, several sons and some charming daughters. Everyone feared that she was going to continue in this pattern for the rest of her life. However, her relatives prevailed on her, and when I returned to Basrah after an absence of more than a year, I found that she was once more modishly dressed, had a fashionable and very becoming hairdo, and had resumed her proper place in society. I never got really close to her again, and I have always thought it was because she felt she had destroyed a picture of herself as the eternally mourning mother. She regretted the fact that she had emerged into the world again, and by so doing had to abandon the role which she would have preferred to continue to the end of her days.

Two widows whom I knew well, both from prominent families, have thrown themselves into welfare work since their husbands died. They have been the moving spirits in a clinic for poor mothers and babies, which has developed into a large and useful organization chiefly through their efforts.

Contact with death in any form is considered to risk bringing great evil upon certain members of society. A bride, or a newborn baby and its mother, should not receive the visit of a person coming from a house where there has been a death, unless the visitor has broken the spell by calling at another house on the way, or at least putting her foot over the threshold of another house. A widow should not come near a bride or a newborn child until a year after her bereavement. If a person has been to a funeral, or had any contact with death, and comes into the house of a mother and baby, they are both removed to another place, preferably a floor above the visitor. If there is a death in a neighboring house, whenever possible the baby and mother are taken elsewhere till the body has been buried.

When my Sheikha friend's daughter-in-law finally produced a son, after several disappointments, I had very recently heard of my mother's death in America. I was longing to see them and congratulate them in person and inspect the baby, but I sent my old Zahra with a message. "Tell them, Zahra," I instructed her, "that I can't come myself because I am 'sad' [the conventional word for being in mourning], but tell them that I thank God for the safety of mother and child, may God preserve them and bless them." She no doubt embellished the message with many variations and repetitions, and did full justice to all the proper felicitations on my behalf.

The Arabic expression when referring to a person who has died is "the one upon whom God has had mercy."

X

Seven-Eye Beads

Bright blue beads with seven eyes, crude and uneven, have always been one of the most familiar of all the many good-luck talismans which are so common in my part of the Arab world. They are sewed on to babies' caps and the back of their little jackets, and are suspended over their cradles. One sees them on the harness of donkeys and camels, and strung up at the front of motorcars.

It is incongruous that a religion founded firmly on belief in predestination and the complete supremacy of the will of God, should have room for the fears and dreads of evil which, at least up to a generation ago, beset the Moslem child and his mother from his birth. He was conscious of a world of unseen beings all around him—angels, jinn, demons, and devils, and his familiar spirit or Qarina—which were to be welcomed and honored, or feared and propitiated.

Angels are very numerous, and in addition to Gabriel, Azrael, Azrafel, and Michael, and the two blue-eyed angels Munkar and Nakir who catechize the dead, every child has two recording angels. They sit on his right and left shoulder and record all the good and evil acts. Mohammed warned his people not to spit in front or to the right, but always over the left shoulder, as that is the side where the recorder of ill deeds stands. There are many guardian angels whose names are written on amulets; eight special angels carry the throne of Allah, and nineteen have charge of the fires of hell. The Koran tells of two angels of Babylon called Harut and Marut who teach men how to bind or break the marriage vow.

The forty-sixth and seventy-second chapters of the Koran describe the jinn, spirits created of fire and of various shapes, who marry and carry on either good or evil till they die. The Koran says that the Prophet Solomon sealed up some of them in brass bottles. These heard Mohammed's preaching and were converted to Islam.

The evil jinn frequent wells, ruined houses, baths, and the mountains of Kaf which surround the world. They love the dark, and one of the first prayers a Moslem child has always been taught is to be delivered from their power. These jinn are of three kinds—those who fly in the air, those who resemble snakes, and others who are like human beings.

The doctrine of devils is equally terrifying. Satan, who is called Iblis, was expelled from Paradise because he refused to obey God's command to prostrate himself before Adam. (Surah: vii, v. 10–17.) He became so angry that a splinter of fire flew off from him and out of this God created his wife. They had numerous and terrible demon children who are workers of iniquity in various ways. One called The Father of Bitterness presides over deserts and causes sorrow; another presides over markets, and causes to look beautiful (in the eyes of men) the talking of nonsense, a false oath, and the praise of merchandise; one called Bathr presides over misfortune, and causes to look beautiful (in the eyes of men) the scratching of faces, the slapping of cheeks, and the picking of pockets.

Closely allied to jinn and devils is the Qarina, each human being's familiar spirit, usually of the opposite sex. This is something that I found even my intimate friends reluctant to mention. All women were fearful of this "double," whose fate was mysteriously linked to their own, and whose wrath they should not incur for fear of vengeance. It was better never to speak of it, but to use all means of propitiation and of warding off possible harm.

There are many passages in the Koran which make it clear that the "double" is a devil—a *shaitan* or jinn—born at the same time as the human counterpart, and a constant companion throughout life. There is a Moslem tradition that the Prophet's Qarina was influenced to become good instead of evil.

Ayesha, his wife, said, "O Apostle of God, is there a devil with me?" To which he replied, "Yes, and with every person."

She asked, "And with you also, O Apostle of God?"

He answered, "Yes, but my Lord Most Glorious and Powerful has assisted me against him, so that he became a Moslem."

Someone else asked him the same question, and he replied:

"I also, but God has helped her so that she does not command me except in that which is true and good."

He is also quoted as saying:

"I was superior to Adam in two particulars, for my devil [Qarina] although an unbeliever, became through God's help a Moslem, and my wives were a help to me, but Adam's devil remained an infidel and his wife led him into temptation."

Moslem Tradition also says that Jesus had a Qarina, but because He was sinless, Satan was unable to touch Him at His birth, and His Qarina became a good spirit, like that of Mohammed. An Arab writer says:

"On the authority of the Ka'ab the Holy Spirit, Gabriel, strengthened Jesus because he was His Qarina and His constant companion, and went with Him wherever He went until the day when He was taken up to Heaven."

Every human being has a Ta'aba—a "follower"—identical in most ways with the Qarina, except that the Qarina sometimes tries to help the human partner if her jealousy is not aroused, and the Ta'aba is wholly malevolent. She is jealous of a human bride or bridegroom. A man's Qarina hates his bride and tries to injure her; a woman's Ta'aba is jealous especially of her child and seeks to injure or kill it. It also tries to part lovers. There is an old belief that the Qarina can assume the shape of a household animal, usually a cat or a dog. The thought that a Qarina might dwell in the body of a cat after nightfall has kept many people from beating or injuring a cat after dark, no matter what the provocation!

There is another shadowy figure of malignancy called the Umm-as-Subyan, the Mother of Children, who is also feared and dreaded.

To these forces of evil have traditionally been attributed all the miseries of jealousy, hatred, and envy; trouble between husbands and wives; sterility and barrenness; death of unborn children; and every sort of illness and unhappiness.

Those who had been in contact with death, birth, and marriage were peculiarly susceptible to malign influences themselves, and were also liable to bring trouble and evil to anyone they met or visited. A bride, a menstruating woman, a woman in childbed, a newborn child, and a person who had been in contact with death were a menace to everyone they met, and in constant danger themselves, until some form of purification had taken place. Sometimes this was a religious rite (as in the case of a newborn baby) and sometimes it seemed more like magic.

The tendency to misfortune or mishap, when not occasioned by the forces of evil, has various names in Iraq. *Chebsa* is a "sudden attack"; *dosa* a "treading underfoot"; and *riha* is effluvium.

Jidda Atiyah was a mine of information to me on all this lore. I told her, in my early days, what a to-do my schoolgirls made about vaccination. This was in Turkish days, before World War I, when there was no Health Service and no municipal sanitation laws. Smallpox was rife, and I thought I was doing my pupils a good service by arranging to have them all vaccinated. The older girls had studied physiology and hygiene, and in theory at least understood the principle and value of vaccination. While they were being "done" by the nurse from our mission hospital (some of them very reluctantly) the little ones, with their teacher, were in the kindergarten room with the door closed. I shall never forget the concerted roar that met my ears when their door was opened. Some of the smallest children were absolutely hysterical with fright. The one word that was intelligible in the chorus of shrieks was "Riha! Riha!" ("The smell! The smell!") I finally elicited the reason—they were convinced that the smell of a vaccination scab, on anyone who had a good take, would give smallpox to everyone else in the house. Jidda Atiyah confirmed this notion to me. She assured me that I was quite right in giving in to the strong prejudice of some of the children, and excusing them from what seemed to them a wholly hazardous experience. In after years, we laughed together over the episode, for an excellent Health Service was begun during the military occupation of Iraq in World War I, and the Iraq government has carried it on with energy and scientific skill. In a surprisingly short span of years, preventive inoculations for plague and cholera as well as compulsory smallpox vaccination came to be taken for granted.

Jidda Atiyah told me, back in this early time, that a woman who is nursing her baby should not go to see the mother of a newborn child, till the latter has paid her ceremonial visit to the bath.

"The new baby might smell the riha!" she said. "It would be sure to have a setback. The only thing to do then, is to put sugar under the armpits of the new mother, mixed with a little water and with milk from her breast, and take this to the house of the ill-omened visitor. She must give it to her own child to drink, and this will break the harmful spell.

"And so many things can cause chebsa!" she continued. "A bride should not meet another bride at the public bath, nor a new mother another young mother. A kiss helps, but more than likely, the mother's milk will dry up or her child take sick, one bride will fail to become pregnant—and then something must be done!"

She enumerated to me all the causes of chebsa or dosa. The first was contact with death in any form, and she described the elaborate precautions to counteract it. Next was contact with a bride, which was equally inauspicious for another bride, or a mother and child, till forty days after the wedding. Ceremonial baths lessened the danger from these causes. The visit of a person coming from the bazaar with purchases was especially dangerous to babies, as Fatima had so graphically described to me.

The visits of a menstruating woman, or one who has not yet visited the public bath after her time of the month, was of ill omen.

Ordinary washing, or an unofficial bath, could cause chebsa, when it should have been a proper ceremonial visit to the public hammam, especially after the birth of a child. The new mother used to break an egg on the threshold of the bathhouse, and again at each door she passed through. In the hot room her friends prepared a mixture of raw egg, wild mint, and cinnamon, and smeared it over her, not to be washed off till she had perspired freely.

A favorite explanation of chebsa was from a sudden fright. An alarming sight, a bad dream, unwelcome news abruptly told, or any other shattering experience, can bring the most dire results. Another cause might be the entrance of a person who was angry, or who came from a dispute—and this (rather strangely) included anyone who had just arrived after a journey, or who was about to embark on one.

A spiteful act, from ill-will on another person's part, could also bring about chebsa. I knew a girl who suddenly and unaccountably on her marriage night developed such an aversion to her bridegroom that she would have nothing to do with him. He was a most attractive young man and a very romantic figure, and no one could understand it. She took off all her bridal finery and her gorgeous jewelry and flung it aside, dressed in old clothes and shut herself in a small room, and became hysterical when her family and friends tried to reason with her. Her new father-in-law, a man of great consequence, honored her by a personal visit next day, and had in his hand a beautiful pearl necklace which he wanted to give her. He had no success either; she cried and shrank away from him in terror and distress.

Mullayas and Mullahs were called into consultation, and after some days the cause of the trouble was discovered. A girl cousin, who was envious of her good fortune, had written the bride's name and a verse from the Koran on a piece of paper and put it in a date tree outside the window of the bridal chamber, with a hearty curse. After this was taken away, and special reading ceremonies performed to counteract the imprecations and remove the chebsa, the afflicted girl became normal again, and all was well.

There are minor occurrences which were considered unlucky—the flight of a crow over a house, especially if it cawed three times; the hooting of an owl; or the barking of a dog. Doughty, in his classic *Arabia Deserta,* mentions the belief that the owl was the spirit of a "wailful woman, seeking her lost child through the wilderness"—in other words, a woman who has died in childbirth.

Against all these evils, the powers of darkness and the many sources of harm that could come to a hapless human being, the Moslem woman sought to protect herself and her family by the use of charms, amulets, and talismans. The seven-eye bead, and anything else blue—a turquoise, or a bit of pottery—were popular and potent. The use of amulets was justified by a saying of Mohammed: "There is no wrong in using charms and spells so long as you do not associate anything with God."

The favorite was a miniature Koran in a case of gold, silver, or other metal. Words written from the Koran on paper enclosed in a small leather case, the names of God or their numerical value, and the names of Mohammed and his companions were all considered efficacious. Then came precious stones, with or without inscriptions: beads; old coins; shells; gallnuts; clay images; the teeth of wild animals; and holy earth from Mecca and Kerbala in tiny bricks or contained in small bags.

The covering of the Kaaba, the shrine at Mecca, is taken down every year and renewed, and the old cloth used to be cut into small pieces and sold for charms.

My friend Nuria, a devoted Moslem and an intelligent and educated woman, came back from Egypt with astonishing tales of the way the most popular amulets were made.

"Just imagine, Om John," she began, "the verses must be written with the greatest care by a man who is really holy, and his diet depends on the kind of charms he is going to write! If he chooses the names of God that are terrible, then he must not eat meat, fish, eggs, honey, and musk. If he is writing the amiable attributes, he is to abstain from butter, curds, vinegar, salt and ambergris. If he intends to use both attributes, he must refrain from such things as garlic, onions and asafetida. And the ink he uses may be saffron water, rose water, orange water, onion juice, water from the sacred well of Zem-zem, or even"—in a hushed tone—"human blood!"

One of the talismans she had brought back was called a Budah. This is a magic square, in which the numbers add up to fifteen in every direction, expressed by the letters of the Arabic alphabet. Some Moslem authorities say that Adam invented the square! But it is usually attributed to al-Ghazali, and it was the foundation and starting point for a whole science of talismanic symbols.

Nuria said she was told that this was used against stomach pains, to render oneself invisible, to protect from the evil eye, and to open locks.

"But one of its best uses," she said laughing, "is to ensure the safe arrival of letters and packages!"

A very popular amulet among Shiah Moslems was called Nadi Ali. It was a silver plate, or one of baser metal, with little bells at the bottom, inscribed with a verse:

> Cry aloud to Ali, he is the possessor of wonders,
> From him you will find help from trouble.
> He takes away very quickly all grief and anxiety
> By the mission of Mohammed and his own sanctity.

The medical profession had some bright particular stars in Baghdad during the golden days of the Khalif Haroun al Rashid, of whom one of the best known was Avicenna. He codified Greek and Arabic medical knowledge, and his work was a standard for hundreds of years. In spite of a distinguished scientific history, there was much in Arab medical notions half a century ago that was anything but scientific. Diseases were said to be cold and hot; and man's body was made up of four elements—Phlegm, Blood, Sweat, and Bile. "God the Most High," says an old medical treatise, "created hot nature and its roots from the action of the earth. Then God created cold nature and its roots. The heat paired with the dryness, and they brought forth the four elements. So man is compounded from these different unions."

Branding used to be a favorite remedy for every sort of ailment. I knew of one person suffering from jaundice who was told first to drink buttermilk with turmeric in it, and then was advised to eat a great many watermelons and to be branded on the left wrist just above the thumb. Stomach trouble was treated by brandings in several places all over the abdomen. One poor woman whose eyesight was almost gone as the result of corneal ulcers allowed her eyeball itself to be branded in hope of a cure. A friend of mine whose eyesight was failing went off to what was then a remote village and was branded on her temples.

Smells were considered to have a direct bearing on illness, as I had learned the hard way from my experience when I had my school children vaccinated. It was a common sight to see a woman with both nostrils plugged up with bits of rag, sometimes soaked in asafetida. An open wound was thought to become much worse if the sufferer smelled anything pleasant or sweet. A woman I knew declared that her infected hand began to pain her immediately when a visitor came into her house who was highly perfumed.

Many herbs were steeped and taken as medicine. Nigella (fennel) and senna (dried cassia) were both recommended by the Prophet, and honey and pomegranates were also supposed to have therapeutic value. A favorite remedy for ulcers and sores was a plaster made of camel fat, dates, and salt. Asafetida was very popular, and evidently the idea was that the worse the medicine smelled, the greater was its efficacy.

Pork is forbidden to Moslems and is the most defiling of unclean foods, but they would sometimes go secretly to a Christian household and ask fearfully for a little "swine's flesh," having been told they must make this compromise with their principles in order to bring relief from some mysterious ailment.

Bloodletting by scarification (scratching to draw blood from a smaller vessel) or by venesection (opening a vein) used to be popular, and was supposed to be especially beneficial in the spring.

Other nostrums not to be found in any pharmacopoeia were water in which the verses written by a Mullah had been washed off; or more unpleasant still, water from a glass held at the door of a mosque by women who asked all the worshipers to spit into it as they came out from their devotions. Then it was taken home and given to the unfortunate patient to drink.

There is an old belief that hair and fingernails contain "soul stuff." The tradition is that man's covering before the fall was the material of which our nails are made. All else was taken away from him, but these were left to remind him of what his covering would be in the next world. Clippings of nails were often wrapped in a piece of white cloth and buried, with the words: "O Satan, this is a safe deposit from us as God is our witness."

Hair is equally sacred and must not be in any way dishonored. The Traditions forbid its sale for the purpose of beautifying women or for any reason whatever. Cuttings from human hair were formerly used by Arab doctors as a powerful tonic, administered by tincture or decoction. Of course the hair of saints had more value than that of ordinary mortals. The Prophet's hairs, both from his head and beard, were carefully preserved and are holy relics.

At the end of the pilgrimage to Mecca, when the pilgrim sheds the Ihram, or pilgrim dress, his head is shaved and his nails cut. He then offers the following prayer:

"I purpose loosening my Ihram according to the Practice of the Prophet, Whom may Allah bless and preserve! O Allah, make unto me every Hair, a Light, a Purity, and a generous Reward! In the name of Allah, and Allah is Almighty!"

After this prayer, a good Moslem is supposed to bury his hair cuttings and nail trimmings in sacred soil.

The hand also has special significance, and representations of it are widely used as talismans. It is made of silver or gold in jewelry, or of tin in its natural size, when it may be suspended over the door of a house. The top of a Moslem banner is often of this shape, and one sees it on the harness of horses or donkeys, or painted on the sides of carts. When a sacrifice is made at a house door, or on the foundation of a new building, someone usually dips a hand in the blood of the animal and leaves the mark on the door or wall, as a protection from evil influences.

There are various methods of divination which I used to see in use in Basrah. One was the sand diviner, who for years sat cross-legged just outside one of the chief banks. His art, or science, was based on astrology, and he was consulted as to a fortunate time to lay the foundation of a building, or to go on a journey, or any other major undertaking.

The most commonly used means of divination was the rosary, in connection with a form of prayer called Istikhara. This was the technical name given to the process of securing divine guidance regarding any enterprise—business, journeys, an auspicious time for a marriage, or any of the great events of life. In the earliest times the practice of Istikhara was by the casting of lots, at first using the Koran itself (bibliomancy) and later by the use of the rosary. The common name given to this in Basrah was to *jerr' kheira,* which roughly corresponds to "taking the omens."

The rosary is grasped within the palms of both hands, which are rubbed together, and the Fatiha is slowly and solemnly recited. Then the user breathes on the rosary, so that the power of the sacred words he has just repeated will go into the beads. He then seizes a particular bead at random, and counts toward the pointer bead, or Minaret. He uses the words God, Mohammed, Abu Jahl (the Father of Folly). This was an adversary of the Prophet, supposedly alluded to in the Koran, Surah: xxii, v. 8. "There is a man who disputed concerning God without either knowledge or direction." When the count ends with the name of God, it means that the request has been favorably received; if it terminates with Abu Jahl it is bad; and if with Mohammed, the reply is doubtful. Others say it is more correct to use the names: Adam, Eve, the Devil. The Adam bead signifies ap-

[157]

proval and the Devil bead disapproval. The Eve bead indicates uncertainty, because woman's judgment is fickle.

A prominent citizen of Basrah, old and wealthy and pious, was said to jerr' kheira in order to make the most trivial decisions, as well as more weighty ones. He was traveling in India years ago, with quite a party of friends and retainers. His private secretary, a young man whose family I knew well, told me afterward an incident in their journeyings. They were on the way from Bombay to Delhi by train, eight or ten people all with first-class tickets, when about an hour out of Bombay the old Sayyid remembered that he had not taken the omens, by using his rosary, before beginning the journey. He at once did so, and received an unfavorable result. Much distressed, he had his whole entourage gather up their belongings, leave the train at the next station, and go back to Bombay. Some days later, when he had an auspicious result to his Istikhara, they undertook the journey again and proceeded to their destination.

The attempt to discover a guilty person, usually after a theft, has a variety of Trials by Ordeal, which have been used, in different forms, in the Near East since the days of Hammurabi.

The first one I knew about at first hand was in the little circle of my old Zahra's intimates. She came to me with a long face one morning and said lugubriously, "I can't go out with you this afternoon, I have to go to the Mullah at Rabat with Salaama and all the rest of our group."

"What for?" I asked.

"The Trial by Bread!" she announced impressively.

I expressed suitable interest and curiosity, and she launched into a long and circumstantial tale. Old black Salaama, a cross-grained widow, reputed to have mysterious savings hidden away, had accused a young woman whose mat dwelling was in the same little alleyway as hers, of stealing a silver bracelet. The young woman hotly denied it, loud recriminations and refutations were shouted back and forth, and presently the two opposing principals agreed to the suggestion of all the women in the neighborhood that they should resort to Trial by Bread. There was a Mullah over in the village of Rabat who was renowned for carrying on such investigations. He would render suitable readings from the Koran, with admonitions, and then give a piece of Arab bread to each one of the crowd, and the guilty person would be unable to swallow it.

So, that afternoon, I was regaled with the sight of a long file of women, abbas over their heads, starting off on a footpath through the date gardens. Poor old Wurda, a harmless soul who eked out a living by selling nuts and dried peas and melon seeds, was hustled along with the crowd, leaving her little peanut stand deserted at the side of the road. She had always been friendly with Salaama, and was apparently needed for moral support. In a case like this the whole neighborhood had to submit to the test.

Toward sunset they all trailed back again and Zahra came over to my house to tell me that Najjia, the one who had been accused of the theft, had swallowed her morsel of bread as well as anyone.

"And the Mullah gave her a good big piece, too!" she added triumphantly.

Najjia was well liked by her neighbors and Salaama was a trial to everyone, so they were all rather pleased at the outcome. Some people were uncharitable enough to hint that Salaama had hidden the bracelet herself, and trumped up the charges just to make trouble.

After the excitement had died down, a few days later, I asked Zahra about the whole matter of Trials for innocence and guilt.

"The first," said she, "is the Oath. This may be taken on the Koran, or by just raising the right hand. It has to be done before the Qadhi. The second"—with gusto—"is Eating the

Cane." This, I found, was the bastinado (beating the soles of the feet) kept up till confession was extracted.

Another was to tie a man to a pole fixed in the ground in the market place, with his hands fastened behind him, and keep him there till he broke down and confessed. Still another was to take a small handful of grains of wheat to a Sayyid. He would pronounce curses over them, and they were then given to the accused person, who would try to swallow them. If he could do so he was innocent, but if he was guilty they would stick in his throat.

"In Kuwait," continued Zahra, "they have a Leavened Dough test. All the suspected persons take a piece of dough and work it with their fingers. Those whose dough works smoothly are innocent. But the one whose dough crumbles— that is the culprit!"

Then she told me of the various tests by red-hot iron—some on the hand, and others on the tongue. One test involving molten lead was especially for women, since their faces need not be uncovered for them to be tested in this way. The lead stiffens only around the guilty person's fingers.

The precise and formal pattern of social intercourse has tremendous importance and significance. So also do the right words and expressions, at the right time. Some of these customs have a religious origin, others are motivated by centuries of tribal and family habits and the social pressure of long usage. They have an importance in everyday living which is so immense that it takes a long time for people from free-and-easy America to grasp the idea and to realize the need of conforming, at least in a measure, to this pattern of formality, if we are to be socially acceptable to the Arabs.

How one is greeted, where one sits, and how one is seen off, all follow a prescribed formula of social etiquette. In general visiting, the host or hostess assigns the place to sit, but even then the visitor, unless he is undoubtedly of higher social rank, does well to sit a little lower than indicated.

When paying a call, the visitor gives the preliminary saluta-tion at the door, "Peace upon you," to which the hostess re-plies, "And upon you be peace." After this, when all are seated, "Good morning" or "Good evening" and other greet-ings are exchanged. Among the many ways of inquiring for each other's health and well-being, my fancy has always been especially tickled by one which is literally: "What is the color of your How?" One's How is a general term in very frequent use, for general well-being, and for mood or inclina-tion. At departure a guest says, "I ask permission to go," "Istarkhus" in Arabic—a word which comes from the same root as a word which means "cheap," *rakhis*. So, by this play on words, the reply is "Ghali"—"You are costly." The hostess will say, "You have honored us," in which case the guest will reply, "We have honored ourselves." After this there is a further exchange of farewells, ending "In the safekeeping of God."

A man never asks after the health of another man's family, as this implies interest in the women, which is unseemly. If I happened to see one of my husband's callers in whose home I might be intimate, I would say, "How is the family?" but I would never mention his wife and daughters by name, unless he took the initiative. If he had a small child, I might inquire for "the protected one" or "the served one."

If it was necessary to give the information that someone was dead, the bald statement was never made. "Your head is safe" or "May you live" conveyed the fact.

When one had occasion to refer to anything regarded as unclean by a Moslem, such as shoe or dog, or to mention any-thing not elegant, like donkey or garbage, the subject was prefaced by a word which implied "excuse me for mention-ing it."

The right hand should always be used in passing anything to another person—for years, I have automatically shifted anything I was about to give to someone from my left hand to my right; it becomes second nature. One always eats with the right hand.

It is extremely bad manners to allow the sole of the foot to point directly at another person.

The traditions, taboos, and observances are believed to have originated chiefly from the Prophet, the Koran, or from the many and varied interpretations in Islamic lore. Some probably come from Greek and Roman sources of great antiquity.

The Chapter of the Forenoon (Sura: 93) has been freely translated by Burton:

I swear by the splendour of light
And by the silence of night
That the Lord shall never forsake thee
Nor in His hatred take thee;
Truly for thee shall be winning
Better than all beginning.
Soon shall the Lord console thee, grief no longer control thee
And fear no longer cajole thee.
Thou wert an orphan-boy, yet the Lord found room for thy head,
When thy feet went astray, were they not to the right path led?
Did he not find thee poor, yet riches around thee spread?
Then on the orphan-boy, let thy proud foot never tread,
And never turn away the beggar who asks for bread,
But of the Lord's bounty ever let praise be sung and said.

XI

Today and Tomorrow

Many were the Ways of Life
That have passed away
Before you: travel through
The earth, and see what was
The end of those
Who rejected Truth.
                    —Koran, Surah: iii, v. 137

When I went to see Fatima's granddaughter, soon after her marriage in 1957, I found her living in a pleasant modern house in a newly developed residential part of town. Acres of date gardens had been cut through and laid out in broad open avenues, and rows of comfortable one- or two-storied houses had been built, each on its own plot of ground. Hollyhocks were already in bloom, a grape arbor was started and so was a rose garden.

After I had congratulated Soheila and wished a blessing on the house, she showed me her new home. She was especially proud of her kitchen, with its electric refrigerator and a gleaming latest-model oil cooking range. The bathroom was also of the most modern type; and there was an air conditioner in the bedroom.

"I'd like a washing machine, too," she said, "but Mama's Kurdish washerwoman is going to come to me one day a week, and she'd rather squat on the back veranda with a row of *tishts* [large round copper pans]. She wouldn't know what to do with a washing machine!

"I've got an electric iron, though," she added. "Everybody knows how to use those now!"

We went back to her living room then and settled ourselves, and I looked around with great interest. This was furnished in simple modernistic furniture, with handsome lamps and vases, a well-filled bookcase; and her wedding photograph with her husband on a small table. Across from it was her graduating picture, in cap and gown, with her diploma from the Beirut College for Women in her hand.

I hadn't seen very much of Soheila since the time she was a baby and then an engaging toddler, for she had gone to Baghdad for her secondary education—the family had usually spent their summers in Damascus or Lebanon—and then for four years she was in college in Beirut.

She had just married a cousin, who after graduating from the American University in Beirut had gone to Scotland and studied medicine. He was now one of the doctors on the staff of the Port Directorate of Basrah, and had specialized in Public Health.

We began with some family reminiscences, gently teasing Soheila's mother about names. Fatima had called her daughter Nejma, which means Star, and she in turn had named *her* daughters Soheila—the feminine for the first-magnitude star Canopus; Zahra, the planet Venus; and Bedrea, which is the Full Moon.

"Fatima," I said to my old friend, "your daughter and your granddaughters are all heavenly bodies! What are your grandsons' names?"

"Shemseddin and Nureddin!" said she laughing. These mean respectively Sun of the Religion and Light of the Religion. "I surely started something when I called my daughter a star!"

"What are the other heavenly bodies doing?" I asked Nejma.

"The boys are still in school in Baghdad," replied their mother. "Shemseddin would like to go into the Air Force, and Nuri wants to take a business course somewhere. And the girls—Zahra was in a Woman's College with Soheila, but she is transferring to the University of Beirut now, because she wants to take the premedical course and then study to become a doctor. And Bedrea, my little Full Moon, is still in school here in Basrah. She will go to Baghdad in a year or two. No one stays at home any more!" she added sadly.

"Well, you went to Baghdad yourself, my Nejma!" observed Fatima.

"Yes, and what a daring and revolutionary thing it was, in those days, and how all the relatives scolded you for letting me go off on my own! I'm sure they thought I would come to a bad end!"

"Times have changed!" remarked Fatima, as grandmothers have been saying since the world began.

"What did you major in at college?" I asked Soheila.

"Euthenics!" she answered. "It's old-fashioned to call it Home Economics. Euthenics means 'The Science and Art of Controllable Environment' or 'The Science and Art of Right Living'!"

"Oh, explain it in Arabic!" begged Nejma. "My English isn't equal to it! And poor Mama"—looking fondly at Fatima —"doesn't understand a word!"

Soheila and I did our best to make it clear to the others what these newfangled terms were all about, and then she continued.

"We each had a turn living in the model home, and shar-

[165]

ing in all the housework; but I liked my work in the Nursery School best of all. I wrote my thesis on 'Child Care in Iraq'; and I am so lucky, I am going to have a job this next year under Sitt Souad, in the new government kindergarten."

(Sitt is the commonly used courtesy title for all educated women now, married or single, though the more formal Saida for the married, and Anisa for the unmarried, are usual on invitations and in written Arabic.)

"I don't like the idea," lamented Fatima. "I want her to stay at home and have a baby."

"I'll have a baby all right, my dear Bibi," said Soheila cheerfully. "I have already decided what I'll name my first girl. Thuraia!" This is the Pleiades, and we all twitted her because she wanted a whole constellation for her daughter, instead of being content with a single star. She took it all in great good part, and then continued seriously.

"In these days we have our jobs as well as our homes. Look at the headmistresses of all the government schools here in Basrah! Every one is married, and Sitt Zakkia, whom I know very well, has a whole crowd of children—so do several of the others. There are woman doctors in the country, too, who are married and have families, and they keep up their practices and continue their clinics."

Nejma now spoke up in defense of her daughter's position.

"My mother," she said deferentially to Fatima, "we should be glad that our girls want to lead useful lives. When I was staying in Baghdad a few years ago, I was really shocked to find what useless existences some of those well-educated young women led. They went to Kabuls [At Homes] day after day, and some of them played poker for hours, in inside rooms, and gained or lost huge sums of money. One of them had been through the Law School, and another had her Teachers' Training Certificate. What an awful waste of a good education!"

"Mama," said Soheila in her turn, "it was very hard on

those girls to come back to Iraq from Lebanon or Egypt where social life was so much more free. Even though they were unveiled, they couldn't go about in mixed company with their husbands; and it was even harder for unmarried girls, especially the ones with jobs, they had to be so *very* circumspect."

"It's a lot better now," continued Soheila. "In Baghdad even more than in Basrah. More and more women are going to the social clubs and enjoying the swimming pools and the tennis courts, along with their husbands and children. They all go to concerts and lectures and the cinema together, too."

"What tremendous strides have been made in women's freedom in only two years!" I exclaimed. I had retired officially in 1955, and had spent more time in Kuwait and Jerusalem than in Iraq since then. It was of deep interest to me, on this visit to Basrah, to hear of the activities of my friends' daughters and my own old pupils.

I had to tear myself away from Fatima and her family, because Waheeda was expecting me. This was a young woman from a very different background. Her father had kept a small grocery shop, and the family lived in a tiny one-storied courtyard house in a populous street near the bazaar. The mother was a Mullaya, who eked out the family living by taking small pupils to learn to read the Koran. The old Bibi, their grandmother, had been for years a special friend of mine; we had become acquainted at Mullaya Medina's readings. Waheeda and her sisters had come to my Thursday club when they were very small, and were clean and well-behaved (in striking contrast to many of our very underprivileged pupils) and were extremely intelligent. We persuaded the parents to send Waheeda and her youngest sister to the government school. The oldest girl was pronounced too grown-up—she was about fourteen—and the following year was married to an intensely conservative husband, who kept her very strictly secluded. Waheeda made excellent

progress, won a regional scholarship to the Teachers' Training College in Baghdad, and now had her diploma and had
returned to Basrah as a teacher. I found her in the same
house; the father had died, the Bibi was old and feeble, and
the mother was about to give up her Koran pupils. The little
courtyard was now neatly paved with tiles, instead of the
dusty mud brick of Waheeda's childhood; water had been
piped in so that they no longer had to go to the neighborhood
pump; and the house was wired for electricity. Waheeda had
fixed up the front room with a dressing table, wardrobe,
chairs and sofas, and a radio. She had the same shining face
and radiated contentment and good humor. She told me all
about her teaching work—gymnastics in one of the large
government schools.

"What about Wuffia?" I inquired with great interest. This
was the older sister with the old-fashioned husband. "Is he
still so strict with her?"

Waheeda laughed. "He will have to break down sooner or
later, because all our friends are going unveiled, but it will
be a hard struggle!"

"Where is your brother Wahbi now?" I asked next.

"Oh, he is in England now," was the amazing reply. "He
is learning to be a river pilot. He got a scholarship from the
Port Directorate. He'll be there another two years."

"And Wafiqa?" checking up on the youngest of the sisters.

"She's still in Baghdad, but she will get her Teacher's
Certificate this year, and already has a job promised her."

"Waheeda," I asked her next, "were most of the girls at
school with you in Baghdad from the cities, or were there
also some from villages in the rural areas?"

"At first, Om John, nearly all were from the cities. Don't
you remember, I got my scholarship because no girls from
Zobeir or Abul Khassib could get permission from their
families to leave home? They really wanted village girls then,

[168]

to train as teachers, but none would come. Now there are more all the time."

"Did you have a chance to see anything of the Village Life Improvement projects out in the country areas?" I asked her, as I had been greatly interested in this new development in social welfare.

"No, Om John, I just didn't have time to visit them," she replied frankly. "I was so busy getting in all my required subjects, I couldn't do anything outside."

I had a lot to think about as I walked home. What a long way Waheeda had traveled, since the days when she had been one of the little gabbling pupils learning the Koran by heart from her Mullaya mother. It seemed like yesterday since she was sitting with the other club children in front of me on the floor, with round solemn face and tight shiny braids, beginning the second stage of her education. Now she was a self-reliant and ambitious young woman, aware of the social problems in her rapidly progressing country. It was heartening to know that a girl of her class, without pull or prestige, could make her way so far through sheer merit and hard work.

Next day I went to spend the day with my Hajjia. We had long arrears of personal news to catch up on, my mouth was watering for one of her delicious Arab meals, and I was particularly anxious to have a good talk with the two young women in the family, her niece and the young half sister (an aunt who was younger than her niece!) who was brought up by the Hajjia, after her parents had both died.

I had paid them a short preliminary call when I first came back to Basrah; and I had been electrified to meet the two young ladies later, in one of the large dry goods shops on a modern shopping street in a new part of town. They wore abbas, but they were unveiled, and greeted me as unconcernedly as though they had been going about in that fashion all their lives. Their brother's car was waiting for them outside with a driver, but otherwise they were unescorted.

"Hajjia, I could hardly believe my eyes!" I exclaimed to her when I saw her at her home. "How did you *ever* give them permission?"

The Hajjia laughed ruefully. "They've been doing it for months, Om John. What else could I do, but allow them to do like everyone else?"

"Hajjia," I asked her curiously, "tell me, does your belief in fate—Naseeb—cover this situation too? In other words, do you feel that God wills that women shall now have their personal freedom?"

"We are all in God's hands!" she replied solemnly. "Nothing can happen to true believers unless it is ordained by Him!"

"Do you think you will ever discard the veil yourself?" I asked my old friend.

"I can't imagine it!" she said firmly. "We old ones don't take to change as easily as the young."

"It comes to us so naturally," said Alia mischievously, "that it seems as though it were meant to be.

"Remember Hafsa?" she went on. "She had practically never been outside Zobeir before, when she went to join her husband in Scotland where he was studying medicine. After she got into the plane at the airport here in Basrah, she took off her abba and veil and threw them down to the people who were seeing her off, and she never wore them again."

"I met her at a party in England that next autumn," I said, "and she was just as much at ease as any of the English girls."

"You'll come to it yet, my sister!" said Alia gleefully.

"God is great!" remarked the Hajjia darkly, and we passed on to other subjects.

We spent some time in recalling an event of several years before which had given us all great satisfaction. Alia had been one of two young women selected to be interpreters for Lady Troutbeck, the wife of the British Ambassador in Baghdad, at a women's party given in her honor on her first visit to Basrah. The other girl had been formally and thoroughly educated in good schools in Basrah and Baghdad, and had also traveled. Alia had studied entirely at home and gained her education through her own efforts. I had helped her with her English for a number of years and she had been an indefatigable and rewarding pupil. She was especially good at mastering idiom and colloquial expressions, and her accent was excellent. Even so, I trembled for her at the prospect of what might be an ordeal, and I was a good deal more nervous than she was before the party.

The Hajjia sat with a group of older women, all in Arab dress, at the festivities, and beamed with pride. I stayed as much in the background as I could, though I was a member of the reception committee, and watched while Alia functioned with the ease and grace of a Junior League hostess. She performed introductions, gave just the right amount of information about the people who were presented, dropped back to allow her co-interpreter to take a fair share of the conversation, answered questions and made explanations, with complete unself-consciousness. Afterward she confided to me, "You know, Om John, I still can't understand how I did it. I never had to stop to feel for a word—the right ones just came without my thinking about it. I even used some words I didn't realize I knew!"

I went back to see Soheila again a few days later, for I had many more questions to ask her about the bewildering changes in the women's world. One of her Beirut classmates, now returned to her home in Baghdad, was visiting her and between the two of them I got many more details.

Fozia, her friend, was particularly interested in rural conditions, as her father came from a large landowning family in the north, though her own generation had always lived in Baghdad.

"Om John," she exclaimed to me, "I was just horrified when I began to go around in the country districts where our family estates are! I was used to the way we and all our friends lived in Baghdad, though of course I have seen the serifa settlements on the edges of the city. But these villages —they are just terrible! The most primitive living conditions! Such poverty, everyone is undernourished, no sanitation, flies everywhere and all sorts of eye diseases, ignorance and apathy—it is those districts that make our percentage of illiteracy so high in Iraq. They say that two thirds of the population live in villages or small towns, or out in the desert."

"But what about the Land Settlement projects, Fozia?" I inquired. "Surely they are tackling this problem, aren't they? Before I left in 1955 the Village Life Improvement projects were begun, too, and Adult Education programs started in lots of rural areas."

"Yes, yes," she agreed, "but there aren't enough of them! And they move so slowly!"

Fozia had spent some of her summer vacations in villages in Lebanon, where her college had conducted summer institutes. She was now going to take some special training as a social worker, under the Ministry of Social Affairs in Baghdad, with a view to rural work. She gave full credit to the voluntary women's organizations operating in Iraq—chiefly in the cities—the Red Crescent and various welfare organizations, though she thought that they ought to be larger and accomplish more! But it was obvious that her overwhelming concern was for the rural districts and the people in the villages.

"What do you know of the work of the Institute of Nutrition, Fozia?" was my next question.

"A very good thing indeed," said she promptly, "if it can

just keep going and accomplish its purpose. It's only been operating since the end of 1955. Most people in our country don't know anything about proper food habits, and so many of them are too poor to buy enough food of *any* kind, to be well nourished. This Institute is to teach people about nutrition through the schools and the village centers, and then to investigate the food resources of Iraq, and see if it can't be made more productive. The Institute has a hospital and clinic for deficiency diseases, and they are doing research all the time."

"Tell me about Home Economics, girls—or Euthenics, if that is what we must call it. Do the schools in Iraq teach it, or must girls go to Beirut if they want special training in domestic science?"

"Oh no, we have it here now!" they said both together.

"In 1952 it was introduced, and now we have a specialized Home Economics college right in Baghdad," continued Soheila. "One of our friends who will graduate next year from Beirut College for Women is writing her thesis on the status of the movement in Iraq. She is getting very interesting reports from a survey she is making, of how widespread the teaching of Home Economics is becoming in our country. I think she said that out of seventy-four intermediate and high schools for girls, forty teach Home Economics."

"They should *all* do so!" said Fozia indignantly.

"There aren't enough teachers," replied Soheila reasonably. "That is one of our greatest problems. And that," she continued, turning to me, "is why girls like me should go on teaching, even after they are married."

"I worked out a course on Family Life," I told them, "for my more advanced club girls. Most of them are illiterate, and they are very apt to be married off at fourteen or fifteen." I sighed as I thought of one of my promising pupils who had disappeared just as she was making such good progress in a special literacy class.

"Well, I am going to be twenty-one my next birthday!" declared Soheila. "And you are already, aren't you, Fozia? And not married yet! A real old maid!"

Fozia chuckled. "I have to wait till my uncle's son comes back from his course in the agricultural college in Egypt. Then he and I have a fine future planned out!"

"What age do most of your friends reach, now, before they are married?" I asked them with much interest.

"If we go to college, seldom before twenty," was the reply. "Lots of our friends marry at seventeen or eighteen, if they don't want any more schooling."

"We don't have to worry about partner wives any more. That practice is almost never heard of among educated people today, with of course a few exceptions. I suppose you knew many of them in the old days, Om John?"

"I certainly did!"

"There is still a lot of polygamy in the villages," observed Fozia.

"And among the poorer people everywhere," contributed Soheila regretfully. "Divorce is frequent with them too, and is often very unjust to the women."

"We should all like to see bilateral divorce laws passed," remarked Fozia emphatically.

"What other work are women doing now, besides teaching and social work?" I asked, changing the subject.

"Well, you know one of the former pupils in your American school here in Basrah has been a broadcaster for years in Baghdad Radio. She has certainly been a pioneer! There are lawyers and doctors, nurses and midwives, journalists and office workers, a few engineers and architects, chemists and pharmacists, and some in business."

"The women engineers ought to make Zobeidah their patron saint!" said Soheila, who had been reading Iraq history. "You know she was the wife of Khalif Haroun al Rashid, and she was the person who had wells and cisterns

[174]

made available for pilgrims, along the whole nine hundred miles between Iraq and Mecca, in the Hijaz."

"She had the waterworks built in Mecca, too," added Fozia.

"Isn't she traditionally supposed to be the original for the storyteller Shahrazad, in the *Thousand and One Nights?*" I inquired.

"I believe so," agreed Soheila. "Another piece of her engineering was a gold tree in her palace, with gold birds who sang by automatic devices."

"How about women in industry?" was my next question.

"Oh yes—spinning and weaving; mats and basketmaking; and brushes and brooms. There are always women working in the bakeries, and some in the cigarette factories."

"Don't forget the Khawat Rezna, here in Basrah!" put in Soheila. "They've been in industry for years!"

We all smiled at the mental picture called up by the mention of these hardy daughters of the desert. They lived in a village of their own on the edge of town, and their occupation was to carry bricks and other building materials wherever construction projects were going on. Like most tribal women, they have never veiled, and they are of fine physique and posture. A row of them swinging purposefully along, with their heavy turquoise and silver ornaments jingling, is one of the most familiar sights on the streets of Basrah.

One of my most satisfying conversations, which took place a few days later, was with a young teacher in one of the government schools. I had heard her chant the Koran with great beauty at a program given in a large Assembly at one of the government high schools, and was told then that she was one of their teachers of religion. The principal of her school was an old friend of mine, so I went to call on her and have a look at her girls and her building, and asked if I could meet the religion teacher. Sitt Saleema had a vacant period and so we sat down together in the pleasant little teachers' sitting room. She was a serious-faced young woman with a serene but somewhat withdrawn air. I found she was from Zobeir, so she was a small-town girl. I plunged immediately into the subject that was on my mind, and which she knew was the reason I had asked for this talk with her.

"Sitt Saleema, with all this modernization, and the very rapid social progress that Moslem women have made, how much place do you think religion still has in their lives?"

She looked thoughtful, and paused for a few moments before answering.

"To some, no place at all, I am afraid!" she said honestly. "To others, the feeling that we should respect it because of its history, but with the judgment that it is old-fashioned and outmoded, and not suited to the present day. Many of us feel a great concern that we must preserve the values of Islam, and train this generation of school children so that they will keep their feet on the straight path."

It was significant to notice how she involuntarily slipped into the language of the Koran.

"We have religious instruction in all our schools, for both boys and girls," she continued. "Would you like to see a copy of our curriculum?"

I said that I would indeed, and she began by reading me the introduction. I was particularly struck by the fact that after emphasizing the need of imparting religious precepts, teaching obedience to orders and abstaining from what is forbidden, a special point was made of the need for character training.

" 'Religious precepts are composed of beliefs, rituals, and behavior, and of character training,' " she read to me. " 'The teacher should not confine himself to filling the child's brain with creeds and rituals and ways of worship—he should rather lay great stress on teaching character, and he should give, for memory work, many sacred verses and traditional phrases concerning character, after he has explained such verses thoroughly.' "

This trend was extremely interesting to me, for the criticism in the past has been that the Koran was taught by rote, and that Moslem children had no conception of its relation to conduct.

I looked over the curriculum carefully and asked Sitt Saleema several questions. There was a detailed program beginning with the elementary schools and going through the intermediate and secondary schools. The relationship of the Koran schools, or Mullah Schools as they were called, was made clear. The Mullah Schools laid special stress on memorizing the Koran and then learning to chant it, beginning at a much earlier age than in the state schools.

"What is the place of the Ramadhan Fast in your lives today?" I next asked her. I had heard broadcasts from Cairo on the spiritual blessings of the Fast, and the physical and psychological benefits, and I wondered how much of this propaganda was effectual in the modern world.

"I think it has a large place," she said thoughtfully. "All over the Arab world, the point is being made that a good Arab must be a good Moslem. You see, Islam is woven into the very fabric of our history and our society. It is a whole way of life. We religious teachers must make it clear that it is not just a historical heritage, but that it has vitality and validity for the present day."

Sitt Saleema impressed me as a really dedicated person, and I detected in her a trace of the mystic element which had been in the character of my great and gifted friend of long ago, Mullaya Medina. But this girl was not living in the past, she was facing squarely the challenge of the present day and trying to meet it.

"Do you think women will ever be allowed to study at al Azhar, Sitt Saleema?" I asked her before we parted. This is the great Moslem University in Cairo which is regarded by many people as the spiritual and intellectual heart of Islam.

"Oh, Mrs. Van Ess, I don't know!" she exclaimed. "You know, every few years there is an agitation about it, and rumors that there is a project on foot to admit women. Then nothing more is heard. The religious leaders are very conservative, and in spite of the progress that women have made, it is still a man's world!"

I left Iraq in 1957, and in 1958 it became a republic. Since then education has had a tremendous impetus, and not only are the regular schools extending their scope, especially for girls, but adult classes have been set up for women who have not before had the chance for formal education. There has been a woman member of the Cabinet in Baghdad, and individual women have received grants of land from the government in rural areas under the Agricultural Reform Law. Plans are under way for legislation to guarantee women's property rights, to modify the laws and usages of marriage and divorce, and to give women a voice in running the country.

Nearly twenty years ago I wrote a statement about the Arab women I had known so well, and ended with a sentence which today, even more than then, has a note of prophecy.

I had been referring to the use of the term Aqila—the "tethered one"—for a man's wife, the same word as that used for a hobbled camel, which had been common when I first went to the Arab world, and which was already beginning to be replaced by Karina, in the sense of "joined."

I went on to say:

The Arab woman has definitely been hobbled in the past, literally by her seclusion in the harem and behind her veil; figuratively by illiteracy, legal and social handicaps, and injustices, and by a complete lack of voice in how her world shall be run. Add to this the low moral level of polygamous society with the physical and psychological evils which result from it, and the odds have been heavy against her. In spite of this, her vitality

[178]

and individuality have been unquenched, her buoyancy and originality invincible. With her roots in a great tradition of the past, with incredibly rapid advance of opportunities in the present, and her rich gifts of personality, who can say what her future may be?

INDEX

Index